ISSUES THAT CONCERN YOU

Recycling

Lauri S. Scherer, *Book Editor*

GREENHAVEN PRESS
A part of Gale, Cengage Learning

GALE
CENGAGE Learning·

Detroit • New York • San Francisco • New Haven, Conn • Waterville, Maine • London

Elizabeth Des Chenes, Director, Content Strategy
Cynthia Sanner, Publisher
Douglas Dentino, Manager, New Product

For more information, contact:
Greenhaven Press
27500 Drake Rd.
Farmington Hills, MI 48331-3535
Or you can visit our Internet site at gale.cengage.com

For product information and technology assistance, contact us at

Gale Customer Support, 1-800-877-4253
For permission to use material from this text or product, submit all requests online at www.cengage.com/permissions

Further permissions questions can be e-mailed to permissionrequest@cengage.com

Articles in Greenhaven Press anthologies are often edited for length to meet page require-ments. In addition, original titles of these works are changed to clearly present the main thesis and to explicitly indicate the author's opinion. Every effort is made to ensure that Greenhaven Press accurately reflects the original intent of the authors. Every effort has been made to trace the owners of copyrighted material.

Cover image © italianestro/Shutterstock.com.

LIBRARY OF CONGRESS CATALOGING-IN-PUBLICATION DATA	
Recycling / Lauri S. Scherer, book editor.	
pages cm. -- (Issues that concern you)	
Summary: "Issues That Concern You: Recycling: This series provides readers with information on topics of current interest. Focusing on important social issues, each anthology examines its subject in a variety of ways, from personal accounts to factual articles"-- Provided by publisher.	
Includes bibliographical references and index.	
ISBN 978-0-7377-6932-6 (hardback)	
1. Recycling (Waste, etc.)--Juvenile literature. I. Scherer, Lauri S., editor of compilation.	
TD794.5.R4196 2014	
363.72'82--dc23	
	2013037151

Printed in the United States of America
1 2 3 4 5 6 7 18 17 16 15 14

CONTENTS

Introduction   5

1. **Recycling Is Necessary and Effective**   10
   David Bornstein

2. **Recycling Is Unnecessary and Ineffective**   17
   Daniel K. Benjamin

3. **Recycling Should Be Mandatory**   22
   Tampa Bay (FL) Times

4. **Is Recycling Worth It?**   26
   Laralyn Murphy

5. **Recycling Saves Resources**   30
   *South Carolina Department of Health and
   Environmental Control*

6. **Recycling Wastes Resources**   35
   Floy Lilley

7. **Nuclear Waste Should Be Recycled**   41
   Gary Wolfram

8. **Nuclear Waste Should Not Be Recycled**   46
   Union of Concerned Scientists

9. **Trash Should Be Recycled into Energy**   51
   Joe David

10. **Trash Should Not Be Recycled into Energy**   57
    Global Alliance for Incinerator Alternatives (GAIA)

11. **Electronics Recycling Does Not Pollute Third World Countries**   **64**
Adam Minter

Appendix

What You Should Know About Recycling   **70**
What You Should Do About Recycling   **75**

Organizations to Contact   **79**

Bibliography   **83**

Index   **88**

Picture Credits   **92**

For decades, cans, bottles, newspapers, and other materials have been the focus of cities' mandatory recycling programs and thus the subject of debates over whether such initiatives squander or save resources and make economic and environmental sense. But in the twenty-first century, a new frontier in urban recycling has surfaced: mandatory composting. Composting—letting organic matter (which includes vegetable scraps, fruit rinds, coffee grounds, eggshells, and other food waste) decompose until it turns into a rich fertilizer—has long been a standard practice on farms, vineyards, gardens, and wherever else nutrient-rich soil is needed. But adding composting to city recycling programs is a new measure, one that has met with both success and opposition.

San Francisco, California, which leads the nation in recycling, was the first American city to make composting mandatory. In 2009 it passed the San Francisco Mandatory Recycling and Composting Ordinance, which requires city residents to sort out their food scraps from other waste or else pay a one-hundred- to one-thousand-dollar fine. Residents are given three bins—one black, for trash; one blue, for recyclables; and one green, for food waste and other compostable materials.

The city reports that since the composting initiative went into effect, compost collection has increased by more than 50 percent and the city collects more than six hundred tons of composted food waste each day. This waste is transported to facilities just outside the city, where microbes eat away at it, breaking it down into a nutrient-rich soil. From here it is sold to a variety of ventures, including the Highway Department (which uses it to fertilize landscaping along roadways) and farms (which grow produce that is sold back to city residents, restaurants, and wholesale vendors). The composted soil is also sold to wineries, which account for much of the region's tourism. "A lot of wineries in Napa and Sonoma [Counties in California] are big buyers of the compost [because] it has [a] high nutrient value,

Former San Francisco mayor Gavin Newsom speaks before signing into law his city's Mandatory Recycling and Composting Ordinance, which requires city residents to sort out their food scraps from other waste or else pay a fine.

so that's a nice way to close out the loop from what we put in our green bins,"[1] says Guillermo Rodriguez, the communications director for San Francisco's Department for the Environment. In addition to having these economic benefits, the city reports experiencing a multitude of environmental benefits, too: The composting program has reduced San Francisco's greenhouse gas emissions to almost 12 percent below 1990 levels and has helped it keep nearly 80 percent of its total waste out of landfills—a rate far ahead of every other city in the country.

Some residents initially balked at the mandatory composting program, in part because it was unfamiliar and also because it seemed messy, even disgusting. "How do you get the bulk of your citizenry that was raised on garbage disposals and anti-bacterial soap to hang on to their avocado pits and sandwich wrappers?" wondered reporter Sven Eberlein. "It's like eating something you've never had before; there's a mental block that's hard to overcome without a little help." Soon, though, mandatory composting became part of people's lives, second nature for San Franciscans. "Trips to cities without composting bins feel like visits to strange planets in distant galaxies," writes Eberlein. "The fact that we could so quickly get used to skittle-sized garbage bags while our compost bags are bulging with leftovers speaks not only to a well-conceived program and the adaptability of San Francisco residents, but to the potential of reaching similar milestones anywhere else in the U.S. or abroad."[2] Based on San Francisco's success, other cities, such as Seattle, Washington, and Portland, Oregon, have also instituted mandatory composting.

In 2013 the city of New York announced plans to follow this model. Then mayor Michael Bloomberg announced he was piloting legislation that would require New York City's 8 million residents to separate food scraps from other garbage and recyclables. Bloomberg believed the measure would save money, energy, and space in landfills. "We bury 1.2 million tons of food waste in landfills every year at a cost of nearly $80 per ton," said Bloomberg when he rolled out the initiative. "That waste can be used as fertilizer or converted to energy at a much lower price. That's good for the environment and for taxpayers."[3]

But many others thought mandatory composting initiatives were a bad idea, fearing the composts would attract vermin and were not a good fit for cramped, apartment-heavy urban living. "We're all for eco-friendly initiatives, but we're really not enthused about the stench of day-old meals wafting through our shoebox-sized, unair-conditioned apartment,"[4] wrote Rebecca Hiscott in the *New York Observer*. Others argued that mandatory composting programs are not environmentally friendly, given the number of trucks—which consume oil and emit air pollution—needed to collect and transport food waste. "There's no way food scraps can be picked up from every home throughout the city without greatly increasing the number of trucks, traffic, and tyranny,"[5] said Jeff Stier, director of the National Center for Public Policy Research. Still others viewed a mandatory composting program—which would levy fines on people who did not participate or participated wrongly (i.e., by putting something noncompostable in a composting bin)—as "the nanny state gone crazy,"[6] as judge and news analyst Andrew Napolitano put it. Napolitano and others complained that mandatory composting and recycling programs unnecessarily impinge on citizens' freedom and should be rejected.

As of January 2014, when Bloomberg left office, it remained to be seen whether America's largest city would adopt mandatory composting. But the idea was gaining traction in that and other metropolitan areas and thus becoming subject to many of the debates and controversies that have swirled around recycling for decades. Whether recycling saves or wastes resources, creates jobs, and is environmentally friendly are among the many topics explored in *Issues That Concern You: Recycling*. Thought-provoking pro/con article pairs will help readers form their own opinion on this relevant topic while fact-filled appendixes provide material for papers and research.

Notes

1. Quoted in Brian Clark Howard, "How Cities Compost Mountains of Food Waste," *National Geographic*, June 18, 2013. http://news.nationalgeographic.com/news/2013/06/130618 -food-waste-composting-nyc-san-francisco.
2. Sven Eberlein, "Where No City Has Gone Before: San Francisco Will Be World's First Zero-Waste Town by 2020," AlterNet, April 18, 2012. www.alternet.org/story/155039 /where_no_city_has_gone_before%3A_san_francisco_will_be _world's_first_zero-waste_town_by_2020.
3. Mayor Bloomberg Delivers 2013 State of the City Address," NYC.gov, February 14, 2013. www.nyc.gov/portal/site/nyc gov/menuitem.c0935b9a57bb4ef3daf2f1c701c789a0/index .jsp?pageID=mayor_press_release&catID=1194&doc _name=http%3A%2F%2Fwww.nyc.gov%2Fhtml%2Fom%2 Fhtml%2F2013a%2Fpr063-13.html&cc=unused1978&rc=11 94&ndi=1.

4. Rebecca Hiscott, "Bloomberg Wants Your Tired, Your Poor and Your Compost," *New York Observer*, June 17, 2013. http://observer.com/2013/06/bloomberg-wants-your-tired-your-poor-and-your-compost.

5. Quoted in Cheryl K. Chumley, "NYC Mayor Bloomberg Pushes Mandatory Composting," *Heartlander Magazine*, July 5, 2013. http://news.heartland.org/newspaper-article/2013/07/05/nyc-mayor-bloomberg-pushes-mandatory-composting.

6. Quoted in FoxNews.com, "This Is the Nanny State Gone Crazy," June 17, 2013. http://foxnewsinsider.com/2013/06/17/'-nanny-state-gone-crazy'-judge-napolitano-reacts-bloomberg's-proposed-composting-plan?utm_source=feedburner&utm_medium=feed&utm_campaign=Feed%3A+FoxNewsInsider+(Fox+News+Insider).

ONE

Recycling Is Necessary and Effective

David Bornstein

David Bornstein is the founder of Dowser.org, a website that reports on social innovation. In the following viewpoint he argues that recycling is both necessary and effective. Bornstein discusses recycling's many benefits—it saves resources, creates jobs, reduces pollution, produces income, and can even help curb global warming. The problem, says Bornstein, is that Americans are not doing enough recycling, or are not recycling consistently. He reports that only about a third of all waste is recycled. In addition, much recycling is done via a hodgepodge of methods, rendering some of it unusable. Increasing the amount and changing the way Americans recycle could therefore have enormous environmental, economic, and social benefits, contends Bornstein. He discusses ways to make recycling easier and more standardized so more people will do it. He concludes that recycling is so important, it must become as easy and routine for people as driving or other near-automatic activities.

W hat if there were something that could create 1.5 million new jobs, reduce carbon emissions equal to taking 50 million cars off the road, cut dependence on foreign oil, increase exports, save water, improve air quality and reduce toxic waste? What if it were low-cost and readily implemented? Wouldn't everyone do it? At a time of wildfires, droughts and persistent unemployment, wouldn't it be a centerpiece of the presidential campaign?

Well, there is such a thing. It's called recycling. You might ask: Don't we already do that? We think we do, but most of the time, we don't. Nationally, only about a third of municipal solid waste is recycled. (In New York City, it's 15 percent.) And, even when Americans make the effort, we frequently make mistakes that contaminate recyclables—throwing that plate of spaghetti in with those newspapers—so that contents of recycling bins become un-reusable and end up in landfills. . . .

The Many Benefits of Recycling

Most people have only a vague idea of the benefits of recycling. When we don't recycle, we waste huge amounts of water and energy, for example. If you recycle just *one* aluminum can every day for a year, it saves the energy needed to run a television for 711 hours, roughly four hours a day for six months (not that I'm advocating that much TV viewing). . . .

Moreover, recycling is great for a struggling economy because it is labor intensive. Recall Economics 101: the three factors of production are land, labor and capital. When we recycle, we switch from land (natural resources) to labor. Recycling needs people to collect, sort, process, compost and prepare materials. Even though two-thirds of the nation's waste goes into landfills, 85 percent of all the jobs associated with waste come from recycling and reuse activities. Recycling creates jobs that won't be sent offshore.

We Need to Make Recycling Automatic

So why don't people recycle more? It's easy to blame apathy, but often people neglect to do the right thing because they're confused. Research on behavior change emphasizes the need to make desired behaviors as simple as possible—removing the need to make decisions, so people act reflexively.

That is why one of the most important environmental fixes taking root today is an initiative to standardize recycling labels. It's only one piece in a complex puzzle, but it's such a central piece that it seems amazing it's been overlooked for a generation.

"For years, with recycling, we've been focusing on trigonometry and forgetting about one plus one," says Mitch Hedlund, the founder of Recycle Across America (R.A.A.), a Minneapolis-based organization that is leading this initiative. She adds: "I go to recycling conferences where the bins say 'Recycle Only' and even the people there have to look inside and ask, 'Should I put newspaper in or just cans?' If it's confusing for people in the industry, why would we expect that the general public will do it?"

Hedlund believes that this problem will not be solved until recycling becomes automatic, like slowing down when you see a stop sign, for all the actors who play a role in the solution—consumers, janitors, building managers, waste haulers. "Imagine what would happen if everyone was responsible for creating their own *stop signs*," Hedlund said. "That's what you have with recycling."

A Standardized Process

R.A.A. has developed a comprehensive set of standardized labels that are being adopted by a growing number of American and Canadian corporations, schools and government entities. They include Hallmark; Monsanto; AOL; Cummins; Koch Industries; Johns Hopkins University; the Army Corps of Engineers; the town of Banff, Alberta; the county of Arlington, Virginia, and potentially the province of Manitoba. (R.A.A., a nonprofit, sells its labels at low prices, to sustain itself, and uses licensing fees to provide free labels to schools and other groups and to develop other environmental solutions.)

Industries often evolve for years before they establish standards. It took traffic engineers decades to standardize road signs. The red octagonal stop sign became the norm only in 1954, almost a

Recycling proponents claim that if a person recycles just one aluminum can every day for a year, he or she would save enough energy to run a television for 711 hours, which is roughly four hours a day for six months.

half-century after the introduction of the Model T Ford. Years of experiments with diverse emergency response systems preceded the 1967 Presidential commission that led to the 911 standard.

The problem with the recycling logo—the chasing arrows—is that it doesn't tell you what to do. Recycling has rules, but they vary across companies, schools, municipalities, churches and restaurants. Many places, for instance, have switched to "single stream" or "commingled" recycling, allowing people to throw

The Environmental Benefits of Recycling

According to various statistics compiled by the University of Massachusetts, manufacturing recycled products requires, on average, seventeen times less energy than manufacturing the same products from virgin materials.

Material	Energy Savings	Environmental Impact	Natural Resource Savings	Miscellaneous Info.
Aluminum	95% energy savings; recycling one aluminum can saves enough energy to run a TV for 3 hours	Reduces pollution by 95%	4 lbs. of bauxite saved for every pound of aluminum recycled	Enough aluminum is thrown away to rebuild our commercial air fleet 4 times every year
Glass	50% energy savings; recycling one glass container saves enough energy to light a 100-watt bulb for 4 hours	20% less air pollution; 50% less water pollution	1 ton of glass made from 50% recycled materials saves 250 lbs. of mining waste (EPA)	Glass can be reused an infinite number of times; over 41 billion glass containers are made each year
Paper	60% energy savings	95% less air pollution; each ton saves 60 lbs. of air pollution	Recycling of one ton of paper saves 17 trees and 7,000 gallons of water	Every year enough paper is thrown away to make a 12-foot wall from New York to California
Plastic	Plastic milk containers are now only half the weight that they were in 1960		If we recycled every plastic bottle we used, we would keep 2 billion tons of plastic out of landfills	Americans use enough plastic to wrap all of Texas every year
Steel	74% energy savings; every pound of steel recycled saves enough energy to light a 60-watt bulb for 24 hours	Every year we create 11.5 million tons of ferrous wastes	One ton of recycled steel saves 2,500 lbs. of ore, 1,000 lbs. coal, and 40 lbs. limestone	Enough iron & steel is discarded in the United States to continually supply the nation's automakers

Taken from: University of Massachusetts, Amherst; Environmental Protection Agency; Steel Recycling Institute; National Aeronautics and Space Administration (NASA); and the Center for Ecological Technology.

glass, paper, cans and plastics in the same bin. (They are later separated at a "materials recovery facility.").

Others have "dual stream" policies. Some separate paper, which is often contaminated by broken glass. Others separate glass, cans or cardboard. More communities are diverting organic waste for compost. And there are recycling streams for electronics, batteries, toner cartridges, yard waste and a variety of construction materials. As a result, the current landscape is a hodgepodge of signs that are scribbled haphazardly and often stuck on bins or walls with Scotch tape. In addition to the lack of clarity, the overall impression is that recycling is low priority.

Hedlund, an entrepreneur who had built her own communications company, recognized the need for standardization after speaking to many people who had the same problem. Corporate sustainability directors said they spent 70 percent of their time just getting people to recycle properly. Companies eager to use more recycled materials in their manufacturing were constrained by supply shortages, contamination and price. . . .

A New Way to Get More People to Recycle

This September [2012], the National Wildlife Federation, which runs a program called Eco-Schools USA, will be introducing R.A.A.'s labels in 1,000 schools thanks to a donation from Kiehls. In 2010, when a group of schools in the Twin Cities implemented a program using consistent labeling (but not R.A.A.'s labels), recycling increased by 47 percent.

In schools across the country, people are trying to create good recycling programs. They end up inventing different versions of the wheel. "Having consistency community to community and school to school helps educate children about what needs to be recycled," notes Laura Hickey, who directs Eco-Schools USA. "If you're a student and you have all the bins labeled a certain way in elementary school and then you go to middle school and it looks completely different, you have to undergo a new learning process."

Standardized labels alone aren't sufficient; they have to be incorporated in education and training. But they are a necessary linchpin to establish consistent communications across all media. If the images on the e-mails, fliers, posters, banner ads, TV commercials, billboards and news shows match the labels on the bins, the message gets reinforced. Over time, it becomes ingrained.

Recycling Is the Start of a New Environmental Era

Recycling, even if done perfectly, also won't be enough to address our environmental problems. Deeper changes are needed of course—rethinking how much we consume, where we live, how we get around, how we design products. But getting people to modify behavior in small, positive ways has proven effective in spurring bigger lifestyle changes. It's a place to start, or in the case of recycling, to re-start. "We need to solve the basic elephant-size problem that involves the general public's experience and perception of recycling," says Hedlund. "It's time for a little simplicity in a very complex industry."

TWO

Recycling Is Unnecessary and Ineffective

Daniel K. Benjamin

In the following viewpoint Daniel K. Benjamin argues that recycling makes neither environmental nor economic sense. He says recycling has been undeservedly cast as an environmental centerpiece of educational and policy programs that promote sustainability and conservation. But, in his opinion, there is little sustainable or efficient about recycling. Recycling benefits from government subsidies (public money that helps it be affordable), which obscure its true cost and savings. Benjamin says that when he takes into account the total cost of recycling, he finds it is more expensive than landfilling waste and does not save a significant amount of natural resources (because of the energy that goes into the recycling process). He therefore concludes that recycling wastes money, has a negligible environmental impact, and should be abandoned as an environmentally friendly tactic.

Benjamin is a senior fellow at the Property and Environmental Research Center (PERC), a public policy institute that takes a market-based (rather than regulatory) approach to improving the environment. In 2003 Benjamin published "Eight Great Myths of Recycling," an influential policy paper that is often cited by those who make arguments about recycling.

More than 30 years after the homeless garbage barge *Mobro 4000*[1] put recycling on the front pages, recycling remains a poster child for many who consider themselves environmentalists. In [my 2003 paper "Eight Great Myths About Recycling,"] I examined whether residential recycling warranted this status. My conclusion was that it did not. Yet proponents of municipal solid waste (MSW) recycling continue to push it, as both a centerpiece of environmental education in school systems, and as a core component of environmental policy, particularly at the state and local level.

I have recently revisited the issue in [my 2010 paper "Recycling Myths Revisited"], drawing on updated evidence and taking a closer look at the arguments. Depending on one's view of the world, the good news or bad news is that MSW recycling makes no more environmental or economic sense now than it did at the time of my earlier analysis. It is instead an activity that yields negligible environmental benefits, and does so at high economic cost. In short, if we focused our efforts on alternative means of environmental enhancement, we could achieve higher environmental quality *and* have more of other goods.

In the course of my reassessment of recycling's virtues—or lack thereof—I had occasion to more carefully evaluate two questions to which I had given relatively little consideration the first time around. First, isn't recycling a crucial element of living sustainably? Second, don't government subsidies to fossil fuel production markedly distort the cost figures against recycling? As it turns out, the answer in both cases is "no."

Consider first the issue of sustainable living. People routinely use the term "sustainable" without telling others what they mean, so I wish to be explicit. I presume the term means that we are responsibly conserving resources for the future. This requires that we pay for the full costs of our actions today—no less, and no more. If we "underpay" for consuming resources, we will consume

---

1. In 1987 the *Mobro 4000* sailed from New York to Central America and back looking for a place to dispose of the thirty-one hundred tons of trash it was carrying.

A 2011 Ipsos poll found that 87 percent of Americans say they recycle, though just 51 percent say they do so on a daily basis. Thirteen percent say they do not recycle at all. Reasons they do not include because they do not know what is recyclable or because it is too difficult to do so.

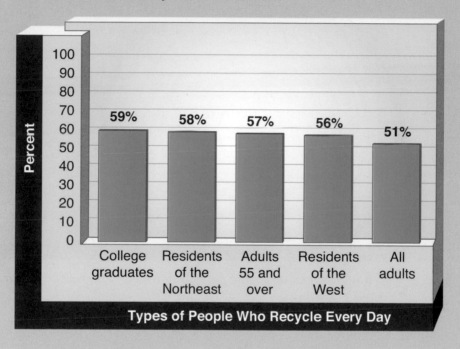

Taken from: "Nine in Ten Adults Recycle, but Only Half Do So Daily." Ipsos, July 13, 2011.

them so quickly that future generations will find themselves worse off as a result. But the reasoning is symmetric: if we "overpay," we *also* harm future generations.

Imagine, for example, that a concern for vistas that might be affected by new wind farms induced us to impose a prohibitive tax (or costly regulatory procedure) on the construction of such facilities. It is true that we would preserve valuable views for the future, but at the expense of inducing us to consume more energy produced by coal. One can easily imagine that the resulting damage to air quality could outweigh the improved views, leaving

The author asserts that recycling costs $120 more per ton than landfilling.

future generations worse off, despite their pristine vistas. The key point here is that to live sustainably we must not only ensure that we do avoid overconsumption; we must also ensure that we do not induce underconsumption.

In the context of recycling, if we want to live sustainably, we must recognize that conserving a few resources (such as bauxite [aluminum ore] or iron ore) does not always constitute living sustainably. We must take into account our actions on the *overall* consumption of resources. My estimates are that recycling costs $120 per ton more than does landfilling—even after accounting for the value of the recycled materials. This implies that MSW recycling programs are counterproductive to sustainable living because they actually waste resources, leaving less for future generations.

But what about those energy subsidies? The production of goods from virgin materials tends to be more energy-intensive than is production using recycled materials. Consequently, it is argued, energy subsidies tend to distort the cost picture against recycling. Well, it turns out that although the *production* of petroleum and coal in the United States is subsidized, their *consumption* is taxed. The net impact on petroleum prices is likely trivial—well under one percent—so that the practical impact of tax policy on the recycling decision is in this dimension undetectable. For coal, roughly 90 percent of the subsidies go toward promoting so-called "clean coal," which has been processed to substantially reduce its pollution potential. Just as importantly, the magnitude of the coal subsidies net of taxes appears to be miniscule [as shown by Gordon Metcalf in "Federal Tax Policy Towards Energy," in *Tax Policy and the Economy*, vol. 21, no. 1, 2007]. The result is that the $120 per ton resource cost disadvantage of recycling compared to landfilling is substantively unaffected by government energy subsidies.

The overall picture that emerges is that mandatory recycling programs create a substantial waste of resources in return for environmental benefits that are questionable, at best. Once we recognize that there are *other* policies (such as a higher national fuel tax) that could yield environmental benefits at far lower costs, we are forced to confront the question: Why are we sacrificing so much to achieve so little? Surely that is a query that proponents of mandatory recycling programs should be forced to address.

THREE

Recycling Should Be Mandatory

Tampa Bay (FL) Times

> In the following viewpoint the editors at the *Tampa Bay Times*, a Florida newspaper, argue that recycling programs must be made mandatory if they are to be successful. They discuss the case of a voluntary recycling program in Saint Petersburg, Florida, which has had minimal success because not everyone participates in it. The editors say Saint Petersburg's recycling program has not generated enough users, making it difficult to run it cost effectively and efficiently. Moreover, the voluntary nature of the program makes it prone to multiple methods of recycling that end up competing with each other, rather than working in concert to recycle items. Recycling protects the environment, makes economic sense, and saves valuable resources, concludes the *Tampa Bay Times*, and is too important to be left up to individuals to do voluntarily.

Less than two years after moving from the dark ages to finally embrace curbside recycling, St. Petersburg [Florida] is on the brink of retreat. A voluntary curbside program run by a private operator has failed to win enough subscribers, prompting some in City Hall to pronounce it just won't work in Florida's fourth-largest city. But that is the wrong conclusion. The real lesson here for city leaders should be that half-measures don't work. The city should embrace mandatory, curbside recycling like that found in other cities in Florida and across the nation to finally move St. Petersburg to a greener and more efficient future.

Successful Recycling Takes Everyone's Participation

As the *Tampa Bay Times*' Michael Van Sickler recently reported, Waste Services of Florida Inc. [WSI] has told City Hall it does not have enough paying subscribers (8,000) to justify renewing its contract with the city this fall. The company had hoped to sign up three times as many households willing to pay $33 a year

Saint Petersburg, Florida, mayor Bill Foster signed a contract with a local waste service in 2010 to provide once-a-week recycling pickup of newspapers, cardboard, aluminum cans, plastic, and glass for a modest price.

for the convenience of curbside recycling. But here is a more telling statistic: The city's 16 dropoff centers—which residents, businesses and nonresidents pay nothing to use—collected nearly 3,400 tons of refuge, twice the amount that WSI did. It's not that St. Petersburg residents won't recycle; it's just that the voluntary recyclers are split between competing systems. And greater recycling collection, along with true economies of scale, won't be

Mandatory Recycling Laws in the United States

Nineteen states require at least one type of material to be recycled. Also, eleven states have "bottle bills," or container deposit laws, in which certain kinds of beverage containers are assigned a minimum refundable deposit.

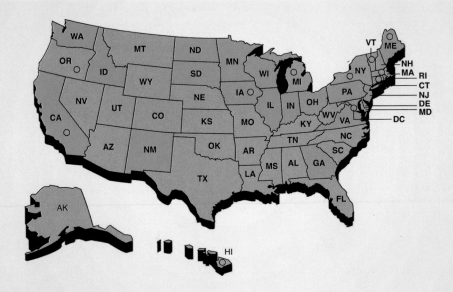

States with mandatory recycling of at least one commodity

States without mandatory recycling of at least one commodity

States with bottle bill

Taken from: "Disposal Bans & Mandatory Recycling in the United States." Northeast Recycling Council Inc. June 24, 2011.

seen until the city integrates more convenient curbside service into waste services.

Elsewhere in Tampa Bay, it isn't this hard. Residents have convenient choices when disposing of trash at the curbside, rubbish or recycling, and most often it is factored into the monthly municipal utility charges. For years, St. Petersburg's discussion was stymied by former Mayor Rick Baker, who questioned its cost effectiveness and the pollution generated by collection trucks.

Mayor Bill Foster deserves credit for finally moving St. Petersburg forward, albeit in half-steps. He signed the contract with WSI in 2010 that provided a once-a-week service recycling newspaper, cardboard, aluminum cans, plastic and glass using a single 18-gallon bin for a modest price. And Foster indicated last week [early May 2012] he would try to find another private provider to keep the service going. That's more enlightened than the musings from council member Jeff Danner, who sounds ready to retreat altogether.

A Proven Method for Environmental Health

But council member Steve Kornell has it right. The city's entire waste management service should be re-examined to see how it might be realigned to support mandatory curbside recycling, which should also allow the closing of some—if not most—of the city's dropoff centers. And it should, over time, reduce the city's waste disposal costs.

Recycling is not the hippy activist cause critics like to claim. It is a proven method to collect valued commodities for a higher use, prolong the life of landfills and protect natural resources. It's also the policy of the state [of Florida], where the Republican-led Legislature has voted twice since 2008 to call for communities to recycle at least 75 percent of their solid waste by 2020. That's eight years away. It's time for the St. Petersburg to get on board.

FOUR

Is Recycling Worth It?

Laralyn Murphy

Recycling programs should not be mandatory, argues Laralyn Murphy in the following viewpoint. She contends that mandatory programs prevent people from knowing whether recycling is actually cost effective, environmentally friendly, and worth pursuing. If everyone is forced to participate and the program has no competition, Murphy maintains, it is impossible to objectively evaluate its strengths and weaknesses. Removing mandates and subjecting recycling to the free market—that is, the business environment in which companies are free to set their own prices and succeed on the strengths and merits of their products and services—is the only way to truly evaluate whether it is an effort worth undertaking, the author asserts. For all of these reasons, Murphy concludes that mandatory programs obscure the true nature and efficacy of recycling and should be ended.

Murphy is a publicity manager at the Independent Institute, a public policy organization that advocates for free markets and against regulations and mandatory programs.

Laralyn Murphy, "Is Recycling Worth It?" The Independent Institute, May 24, 2010. Published by permission of The Independent Institute.

When it comes to absolving your conscience and saving the planet, recycling is a quintessential penance. For anyone suffering from eco-apathy, many jurisdictions make the choice for you, with mandatory recycling and other regulations. Such mandates, however, keep us from knowing whether recycling is cost effective.

Environmentalists claim that recycling consumes less energy and destroys fewer natural resources than original production. For example, recycling aluminum supposedly requires 95 percent less energy than virgin production.

Studies that produce such statistics, though, make many assumptions about human behavior. Government-mandated recycling programs hide costs, rendering the net economic and environmental benefits unknowable. How much energy, for example, was consumed in the collection and handling of the used materials?

Government interference alters the market structure in many ways. California and 10 other states, including Oregon and New York, add surcharges to the price of beverage containers to encourage consumers to take them to recycling collection facilities. Policymakers also create demand for recycling through "minimum recycled content" requirements and by purchasing recycled materials for public projects.

The problem is that all this meddling distorts the market, artificially increasing demand while blurring costs. It's probably safe to say that an aluminum soda can is not worth exactly 5 cents—the standard redemption value in the 11 states with "bottle laws." Studies indicate a real value of about a penny. The arbitrary nickel redemption deposit merely reflects how much the legislature values a certain behavior.

Environmentalists tend to assume that without their efforts everything would be bound for landfills or incineration. That's why they favor forced eco-friendliness.

They forget that the world is filled with other incentives.

A business, for example, would look at the costs and ask simply whether recycling is a viable low-cost production option, all else being equal. If the cost of collecting and remanufacturing aluminum

The author claims that mandated recycling's costs cannot be known until the mandate is lifted.

cans is less than the cost of mining ore and manufacturing new cans, businesses can be trusted to actively promote recycling.

When decisions are based on information from free markets, prices act as unifying language between producers and consumers. Compulsory recycling and price-fixing short-circuit this process, making accurate judgments about the merits of one production option versus another impossible.

Using regulation to alter prices—either directly or indirectly, by politically manipulating demand—replaces a healthy economy with a Tower of Babel. Five cents no longer means 5 cents: It merely represents the power of special interests to force compliance with a politically favored behavior.

Eliminating mandatory recycling, deposit laws and other regulations and subsidies would enable entrepreneurs to freely respond to market signals, prompting competitive efficiency as well as individual responsibility.

It's certainly possible that recycling is as beneficial as environmentalists claim. But because we lack perfect knowledge of every factor of production, profit margins—not politics—should determine if and how recycling is a part of the equation.

FIVE

Recycling Saves Resources

South Carolina Department of Health and Environmental Control

In the following viewpoint the South Carolina Department of Health and Environmental Control reviews the environmental benefits of recycling. Recycling saves natural resources such as oil, water, coal, and other raw materials and eliminates the need to make products from raw materials, which cuts down on the pollution involved in creating, processing, and moving them, the author claims. In addition to reducing pollution, recycling can reduce climate change, contends the author. Furthermore, the department adds, recycling saves energy because creating products from recycled items uses less energy than creating them from scratch. Finally, recycling trash saves space in landfills and contributes to the development of new, environmentally friendly products, the author maintains. For all of these reasons, the department concludes that recycling saves resources and is environmentally friendly.

The mission of the South Carolina Department of Health and Environmental Control is to protect the health of the public and the environment.

Recycling is good for the environment, human health and the economy. And it all starts with you.

The recyclables that you place in your curbside bin or take to the drop-off center begin a ripple effect of benefits. To start with, recyclables have value. By turning waste into valuable raw materials, recycling creates jobs, builds more competitive manufacturing and adds significantly to the nation's economy.

Recycling also promotes the sustainable use of our natural resources. Recycling saves energy. Recycling reduces pollution. Recycling, in short, is working.

There are many environmental and health benefits associated with recycling according to the National Recycling Coalition.

When one ton of steel is recycled, 2,500 pounds of iron ore, 1,400 pounds of coal, and 120 pounds of limestone are conserved.

Recycling reduces the need to build landfills and incinerators. Typically, no one wants a landfill or incinerator built in his or her community.

Recycling Saves Natural Resources and Curbs Pollution

Recycling saves natural resources. When one ton of steel is recycled, for example, 2,500 pounds of iron ore, 1,400 pounds of coal and 120 pounds of limestone are conserved. Recycled paper supplies more than 37 percent of the raw materials used to make new paper products in the U.S. Without recycling, this material would come from trees.

Recycling reduces or eliminates pollution by reducing the need to extract, move and process raw materials. In the United States, processing minerals contributes almost half of all reported toxic emissions from industry, sending 1.5 million tons of pollution into the air and water each year. Recycling can significantly reduce these emissions. Recycling results in a net reduction in 10 major categories of air pollutants and eight major categories of water pollutants.

Recycling Saves Energy and Prevents Climate Change

Manufacturing products from recycled materials saves energy. It takes 95 percent less energy to make aluminum from recycled aluminum than it does to make it from virgin materials. It takes 60 percent less energy to make recycled steel, 40 percent less to make recycled newspaper or recycled glass, and 70 percent less energy to make recycled plastics. These savings far outweigh the energy created as a by-product of incineration or disposing of the materials in a landfill.

Recycling helps reduce our reliance on foreign oil. Recycling helps by saving energy. *Waste prevention and recycling can result in significant reductions in greenhouse gas emissions.* South Carolina recycled 1,229,100 tons of municipal solid waste in fiscal year

Recycling Saves Energy and Reduces Greenhouse Gases

Using the Environmental Protection Agency's Durable Goods Disposal Calculator, the Institute of Scrap Recycling Industries estimates that reduction of carbon dioxide (CO_2) emissions from scrap recycling globally is approximately 500 million tons per year. Consider the energy and gas reductions that are yielded by recycling the following materials:

Recycling	Saves the energy equivalent of:	Reduces greenhouse gas emissions by (CO_2 equivalent):
One car	502 gallons of gasoline	8,811 lbs.
One refrigerator	36 gallons of gasoline	566 lbs.
One computer and CRT Monitor	27 gallons of gasoline	404 lbs.
One washing machine	24 gallons of gasoline	397 lbs.
Four tires	18 gallons of gasoline	323 lbs.
One television	8 gallons of gasoline	81 lbs.
10 lbs. of aluminum cans	7 gallons of gasoline	16 lbs.

Taken from: The Institute of Scrap Recycling Industries (ISRI), 2013.

2012 (July 1, 2011 to June 30, 2012). This results in an environmental impact equivalent to: eliminating emissions from the electricity use of 434,227 homes for one year; conserving 12,463 railcars of coal; or conserving 325,183,632 gallons of gasoline.

Recycling reduces greenhouse gas emissions. Recycling helps reduce greenhouse gas emissions (e.g., carbon dioxide and methane) that may contribute to global climate change by (1) decreasing the energy needed to make products from virgin materials and thereby reducing the burning of fossil fuels (2) reducing emissions from landfills and incinerators, which are major sources of methane gas emissions and (3) slowing the harvest of trees thereby maintaining the carbon dioxide storage benefit provided by trees.

A national recycling rate of 30 percent reduces greenhouse gas emissions as much as removing nearly 25 million cars from the road for one year.

Turning Trash into Products

Recycling stimulates the development of green technology. Recycling allows for and encourages the development of more environmentally friendly products. The vast supply of low-cost recyclables from local collection programs has spurred many businesses to develop cutting-edge technologies and products. Waste tires, for example, are used in many applications including rubberized asphalt for paving roads.

SIX

Recycling Wastes Resources

Floy Lilley

Recycling wastes resources and causes pollution, argues Floy Lilley in the following viewpoint. Recycling is often justified on the grounds that landfill space is at a premium, but Lilley contends that landfills actually have plenty of room and will not be filled up for decades, even centuries, so recycling offers no environmental benefits in that regard. She also contends that recycling is not environmentally friendly because the process uses vast amounts of energy, causes pollution, and requires resources. Trucks that pick up recyclables burn fuel and cause air pollution, for example; recycling items like glass, paper, and plastic takes a lot of water and energy. Given that we are not running out of room for trash and that recycling leaves its own environmental footprint, Lilley concludes it does not save resources and is not environmentally friendly.

Lilley is an adjunct scholar at the Ludwig von Mises Institute, a think tank that promotes free market economics, human independence, and minimal government intervention.

Floy Lilley, "Three Myths About Trash," *Mises Daily*, December 2, 2009. Copyright © 2009 by Ludwig von Mises Institute. All rights reserved. Reproduced by permission.

There are three things everybody knows when we talk trash:

1. We know we're running out of landfill space;
2. We know we're saving resources and protecting the environment by recycling; and
3. We know no one would recycle if they weren't forced to.

Let's look at these three things we think we know. Are they real or are they rubbish? . . .

Landfills Have Plenty of Room

Obviously, and as usual, the real landfill problem is not a landfill problem at all but a political problem. "Fears about the effects of landfills on the local environment have led to the rise of the not-in-my-back-yard (NIMBY) syndrome, which has made permitting facilities difficult. Actual landfill capacity is not running out."

Today, 1,654 landfills in 48 states take care of 54 percent of all the solid waste in the country. One-third of them are privately owned. The largest landfill, in Las Vegas, received 3.8 million tons during 2007 at fees within the national range of $24 to $70 per ton. Landfills are no longer a threat to the environment or public health. State-of-the-art landfills, with redundant clay, plastic liners, and leachate collection systems, have now replaced all of our previously unsafe dumps.

More and more landfills are producing pipeline-quality natural gas. Waste Management plans to turn 60 of their waste sites into energy facilities by 2012. The new plants will capture methane gas from decomposing landfill waste, generating more than 700 megawatts of electricity, enough to power 700,000 homes.

Holding all of America's garbage for the next one hundred years would require a space only 255 feet high or deep and 10 miles on a side. Landfills welcome the business. Forty percent of what we *recycle* ends up there anyway. We are not running out of landfill space.

Recycling Is Expensive and Does Not Save Resources

What are the costs in energy and material resources to recycling as opposed to landfill disposal, which we've just looked at? Which method of handling solid waste uses the least amount of resources as valued by the market?

As government budgets tighten and the cost of being "green" rubs against the reality of rising taxes, recycling coordinators . . . will increasingly be under pressure to justify their programs as cost-effective alternatives to waste-disposal methods like landfills. . . .

Overall, curbside recycling's costs run between 35 percent and 55 percent more than other *recycling* methods, because it uses huge amounts of capital and labor per pound of material recycled.

Recycling Is Very Expensive

The author contends that recycling is more expensive than other waste-disposal methods. The following table shows the cost of handling trash through three different methods. Recycling opponents argue its cost cannot be justified because its positive environmental impact is negligible.

Costs of Alternative Municipal Solid Waste Programs
(2009 dollars per ton)

Program	Disposal	Baseline Recycling	Extended Recycling
Landfill	$36	$0	$50
Collection and transportation	$83	$185	$151
Recyclables processing	$0	$113	$88
SUBTOTAL	**$119**	**$298**	**$239**
Less: Recovery	-$0	-$55	-$40
TOTAL	**$119**	**$243**	**$199**

Taken from: Daniel K. Benjamin. "Recycling Myths Revisited." PERC Policy Series no. 47, 2010.

Recycling itself uses three times more resources than does depositing waste in landfills. . . .

The Solid Waste Association of North America found that, of the six communities involved in a particular study, *all but one* of the curbside recycling programs, and *all* the composting operations and waste-to-energy incinerators, increased the cost of waste disposal. Indeed, the price for recycling tends to soar far higher than the combined costs of manufacturing raw materials from virgin sources and dumping rubbish into landfills.

Recycled newspapers must be deinked, often with chemicals, creating sludge. Even if the sludge is harmless, it too must be disposed of. Second, recycling more newspapers will not necessarily preserve trees, because many trees are grown specifically to be made into paper. The amount of new growth that occurs each year in forests exceeds by a factor of 20 the amount of wood and paper that is consumed by the world each year. Wherever private-property rights to forests are well-defined and enforced, forests are either stable or growing.

Glass is made from silica dioxide—that's common beach sand—the most abundant mineral in the crust of the earth. Plastic is derived from petroleum byproducts after fuel is harvested from the raw material. Recycling paper, glass, or plastic is usually not justified compared to the virgin prices of these materials. . . .

Recycling Causes Pollution

In light of these facts, how can San Franciscans [who have mandatory recycling] and others think recycling conserves resources? First, many states and local communities subsidize recycling programs, either out of tax receipts or out of fees collected for trash disposal. Thus the bookkeeping costs reported for such programs are far less than their true resource costs to society. Also, observers sometimes erroneously compare relatively high-cost, twice a *week* garbage pickup with relatively low-cost, once or twice a *month* recycling pickups, which makes recycling appear more attractive.

Why do these same people think that recycling is protecting the environment by not polluting? Recycling *is* a manufacturing

There are 1,654 landfills in forty-eight states handling 54 percent of all the solid waste in the nation.

process, and therefore it too has environmental impact. The US Office of Technology Assessment says that it is "usually *not clear* whether secondary manufacturing such as recycling produces *less pollution* per ton of material processed than primary manufacturing processes."

Increased pollution by recycling is particularly apparent in the case of curbside recycling. Los Angeles has estimated that its fleet of trucks is twice as large as it otherwise would be—800 versus 400 trucks. This means more iron ore and coal mining, more steel and rubber manufacturing, more petroleum extracted and refined for fuel—and of course all that extra air pollution in the Los Angeles basin as the 400 added trucks cruise the curbs.

Manufacturing paper, glass, and plastic from recycled materials uses appreciably more energy and water, and produces as much or more air pollution, as manufacturing from raw materials does. Resources are not saved and the environment is not protected.

Items of Value Should Be Recycled—
Everything Else Is Garbage

If all we knew about recycling was what we heard from environmentalist groups, recycling would seem to be the philosophy that everything is worth saving except your own time and money. Costs of recycling are mostly hidden. If we add in the weekly costs of sorting out items, it makes more sense to place everything in landfills.

But *private* recycling is the world's second oldest, if not the oldest, profession. Recyclers were just called *scavengers*. Everything of value has always been recycled. You will automatically know that something is of value when someone offers to buy it from you, or you see people picking through your waste or diving into dumpsters.

Aluminum packaging has never been more than a small fraction of solid waste, because metals have value. Ragpickers separating out cloth from waste may not be in season now, but cardboard, wood, and metals have always been in some demand.

Scrapyards recycle iron and steel because making steel from virgin iron and coal is more expensive. Members of the Institute of Scrap Recycling Industries recycle 60 million tons of ferrous [iron-based] metals, 7 million tons of nonferrous metals, and 30 million tons of waste paper, glass, and plastic each year—an amount that dwarfs that of *all* government (city, county, and state) recycling programs.

Recycling is a long-practiced, productive, indeed essential, element of the market system. Informed, *voluntary* recycling conserves resources and raises our wealth, enabling us to achieve valued ends that would otherwise be impossible. So yes, people do recycle even when they are not forced to do so.

However, *forcing* people to recycle makes society worse off. Mandated recycling exists mainly because there is plenty of money to be made by labeling products as "green" or "recycled" to get municipal and federal grants.

SEVEN

Nuclear Waste Should Be Recycled

Gary Wolfram

The United States should recycle its used nuclear fuel, argues Gary Wolfram in the following viewpoint. Wolfram says that multibillion-dollar efforts to store used nuclear fuel are a waste of time, money, and energy. There is still much untapped energy in used nuclear fuel; recycling it could yield further power. In fact, Wolfram contends, as much as 95 percent of used nuclear fuel could be recycled into more energy. Doing so would not only save energy and resources, but also cut down on the costs associated with safely storing nuclear waste. Wolfram points out that many countries—including France, Great Britain, Germany, and Japan—have safely and cost effectively recycled their nuclear waste. He maintains that the United States should do the same so it can save money and energy and lead the world in this important energy innovation.

Wolfram is an economics professor at Hillsdale College in Michigan and the president of Hillsdale Policy Group, a consulting firm that focuses on public policy and taxation issues.

Michigan consumers have paid fees of one tenth of a cent per kilowatt hour of electricity since passage of the Nuclear Waste Policy Act of 1982 to fund the disposal of used nuclear fuel. A total of $540 million has been paid into the U.S. Nuclear Waste Fund by Michigan users of nuclear-generated electricity over the past three decades.

Wondering What Is Going On

Nationally, payments to the waste fund, with interest, have climbed to about $33 billion. Of this, about $10 billion has been spent on developing an underground storage facility for nuclear waste at Yucca Mountain in Nevada.

Plans called for that facility to store waste from commercial nuclear plants such as Fermi 2 and Palisades as well as the defense program. However, the Barack Obama Administration, at the strong behest of Senate Majority Leader Harry Reid of Nevada, halted construction of the repository and directed the Department of Energy to study alternative solutions.

If you are a consumer of electricity in Michigan or elsewhere in the country, you might wonder what in the world is going on. After 27 years and $10 billion spent on scientific research, preparation of a site for the repository and actual construction of a tunnel beneath the Nevada desert, your government has decided this might have been the wrong solution.

Most Used Nuclear Fuel Can Be Recycled

Actually, there is a kernel of truth there. What the United States should do is adopt the same solution to the nuclear waste problem that France and most other countries with nuclear power programs have taken: the recycling of used nuclear fuel. This, along with the construction of more nuclear power plants, on top of the 104 plants now operating, would put the United States back at the head of the international nuclear table. And it would go a long way toward resolving the waste problem.

The amount of used nuclear fuel currently in storage in this country is not an enormous amount by volume. It could be stacked

High Support for Nuclear Waste Recycling

A 2010 international poll conducted by the company TNS Sofres found that the majority of those who are informed about nuclear power issues support recycling used nuclear fuel. Reasons to do so included to save uranium, reduce the volume and toxicity of nuclear waste, and to recover energy.

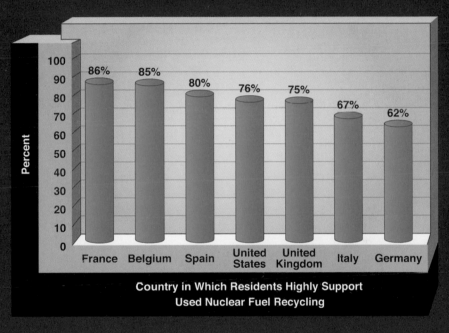

Taken from: "Polls Show Support for Nuclear, But Waste Concerns." *World Nuclear News*, March 23, 2010.

on one football field to a height of 10 feet, and this used nuclear fuel is being stored safely and securely in engineered water pools and dry casks at nuclear plant sites.

However, it is important to recognize that 95 percent of the used nuclear fuel could be recycled.

Other Nations' Success

In fact, countries that recycle their used fuel include France, Great Britain, Russia, Germany, Belgium and Japan. Instead of continuing to store 65,000 tons of used fuel at nuclear plant sites, we should turn the Yucca Mountain site into a national recycling center.

Recycling, also known as reprocessing, reduces the volume of so-called nuclear waste by 97 percent. France, which recycles its

A nuclear waste container awaits recycling. The author claims that as much as 95 percent of used nuclear fuel could be recycled into other forms of energy.

used fuel, obtains about 80 percent of its electricity from nuclear power. All of the nuclear waste remaining from 30 years of nuclear power operations is stored in steel cylinders beneath the floor of one room at a national storage facility in southern France.

It's absurd to treat valuable used fuel as if it's waste. Instead of storing the used fuel in de facto repositories at nuclear plants, as is now done, we should be recycling it for further use. The technology for recycling was actually developed in the United States at Oak Ridge National Laboratory in Tennessee during World War II.

Leading the Nuclear Waste Recycling Movement

Interestingly, there is no U.S. ban on recycling used fuel from the defense program. A recycling facility at the Savannah River Site in South Carolina is nearing completion. Eventually, it will be used to recycle plutonium from the nuclear weapons stockpile into mixed oxide fuel for use at nuclear power plants to generate electricity.

The United States has let other countries take the lead in the development of nuclear power, the energy source that provides 70 percent of our country's carbon-free electricity. Several countries, including France, have built breeder reactors. While France's Super Phoenix breeder has the capacity to produce 1.2 megawatts of power, the U.S. nuclear program is still playing catch-up, for lack of a political consensus on nuclear waste.

Rather than bury our heads in the sand, we should use the Nuclear Waste Fund to improve recycling technology and to develop our own recycling plant. This would be a major step in returning the U.S. to global leadership in nuclear energy.

EIGHT

Nuclear Waste Should Not Be Recycled

Union of Concerned Scientists

> The Union of Concerned Scientists (UCS) is a nonprofit
> organization comprising scientists who promote respon-
> sible, safe, and sustainable scientific solutions to society's
> problems. In the following viewpoint UCS presents sev-
> eral reasons why nuclear waste should not be recycled:
> (1) it would increase the risk of nuclear terrorism—stored
> used nuclear fuel is very safe and not likely to be stolen
> or reused, but used nuclear fuel bound for recycling is still
> volatile and vulnerable to theft; (2) recycling nuclear
> fuel would not eliminate the need to store it but, rather,
> would just require a more complicated storing process; (3)
> technologies and methods for storing nuclear waste are
> much less expensive than technologies and methods for
> recycling it. For all of these reasons the UCS concludes
> that it is unwise to recycle nuclear waste.

Reprocessing is a series of chemical operations that separates
plutonium and uranium from other nuclear waste contained
in the used (or "spent") fuel from nuclear power reactors. The
separated plutonium can be used to fuel reactors, but also to make
nuclear weapons. In the late 1970's, the United States decided on

nuclear non-proliferation grounds not to reprocess spent fuel from U.S. power reactors, but instead to directly dispose of it in a deep underground geologic repository where it would remain isolated from the environment for at least tens of thousands of years.

While some supporters of a U.S. reprocessing program believe it would help solve the nuclear waste problem, reprocessing would not reduce the need for storage and disposal of radioactive waste. Worse, reprocessing would make it easier for terrorists to acquire nuclear weapons materials, and for nations to develop nuclear weapons programs.

An Increased Risk of Nuclear Terrorism

Less than 20 pounds of plutonium is needed to make a simple nuclear weapon. If the plutonium remains bound in large, heavy, and highly radioactive spent fuel assemblies (the current U.S. practice), it is nearly impossible to steal. In contrast, separated plutonium is not highly radioactive and is stored in a concentrated powder form. Some claim that new reprocessing technologies that would leave the plutonium blended with other elements, such as neptunium, would result in a mixture that would be too radioactive to steal. This is incorrect; neither neptunium nor the other elements under consideration are radioactive enough to preclude theft. Most of these other elements are also weapon-usable.

Moreover, commercial-scale reprocessing facilities handle so much of this material that it has proven impossible to keep track of it accurately in a timely manner, making it feasible that the theft of enough plutonium to build several bombs could go undetected for years.

A U.S. reprocessing program would add to the worldwide stockpile of separated and vulnerable civil plutonium that sits in storage today, which totaled roughly 250 metric tons as of the end of 2009—enough for some 30,000 nuclear weapons. Reprocessing the U.S. spent fuel generated to date would increase this by more than 500 metric tons.

U.S. reprocessing would undermine the U.S. goal of halting the spread of fuel cycle technologies that are permitted under the

Nuclear Non-Proliferation Treaty but can be used to make nuclear weapons materials. The United States cannot credibly persuade other countries to forgo a technology it has newly embraced for its own use. Although some reprocessing advocates claim that new reprocessing technologies under development will be "proliferation resistant," they would actually be more difficult for international inspectors to safeguard because it would be harder to make precise measurements of the weapon-usable materials during and after processing. Moreover, all reprocessing technologies are far more proliferation-prone than direct disposal.

Hurting U.S. Nuclear Waste Management Efforts

First, there is no spent fuel storage crisis that warrants such a drastic change in course. Hardened interim storage of spent fuel in dry casks is an economically viable and secure option for at least fifty years.

Second, reprocessing does not reduce the need for storage and disposal of radioactive waste, and a geologic repository would still be required. Plutonium constitutes only about one percent of the spent fuel from U.S. reactors. After reprocessing, the remaining material will be in several different waste forms, and the total volume of nuclear waste will have been increased by a factor of twenty or more, including low-level waste and plutonium-contaminated waste. The largest component of the remaining material is uranium, which is also a waste product because it is contaminated and undesirable for reuse in reactors. Even if the uranium is classified as low-level waste, new low-level nuclear waste facilities would have to be built to dispose of it. And to make a significant reduction in the amount of high-level nuclear waste that would require disposal, the used fuel would need to be reprocessed and reused many times with an extremely high degree of efficiency—an extremely difficult endeavor that would likely take centuries to accomplish.

Finally, reprocessing would divert focus and resources from a U.S. geologic disposal program and hurt—not help—the U.S. nuclear waste management effort. The licensing requirements

Countries That Recycle Nuclear Waste

As of 2012 just five countries routinely recycled significant amounts of nuclear waste, though some countries—such as Belgium—send their nuclear waste to other countries—like France—to be recycled.

Taken from: World Nuclear Association, May 2012.

for the reprocessing, fuel fabrication, and waste processing plants would dwarf those needed to license a repository, and provide additional targets for public opposition. What is most needed today is a renewed focus on secure interim storage of spent fuel and on gaining the scientific and technical consensus needed to site a geological repository.

A Very Costly Process

Reprocessing and the use of plutonium as reactor fuel are also far more expensive than using uranium fuel and disposing of the spent fuel directly. In the United States, some 60,000 tons of nuclear waste have already been produced, and existing reactors add some 2,000 metric tons of spent fuel annually. The Energy Department recently released an industry estimate that a reprocessing plant with

This nuclear-fuel reprocessing plant is in France. The US Department of Energy estimates that a reprocessing plant with an annual capacity to reprocess two thousand metric tons of spent fuel would cost up to $20 billion to build—and the country would need two of these to reprocess all its spent nuclear fuel.

an annual capacity of 2,000 metric tons of spent fuel would cost up to $20 billion to build—and the U.S. would need two of these to reprocess all its spent fuel. An Argonne National Laboratory scientist recently estimated that the cost premium for reprocessing spent fuel would range from 0.4 to 0.6 cents per kilowatt-hour—corresponding to an extra $3 to $4.5 billion per year for the current U.S. nuclear reactor fleet. The American public would end up having to pay this charge, either through increased taxes or higher electricity bills.

NINE

Trash Should Be Recycled into Energy

Joe David

In the following viewpoint Joe David argues that ordinary household trash can be recycled into a valuable fuel source. He explains that although turning garbage into fuel has long been the realm of science fiction, new technologies allow trash to be processed into energy in a clean, cost-effective, and resource-efficient manner. Converting trash to energy requires little energy, does not produce additional pollution, and makes good use of an otherwise useless product, he contends. In addition, turning America's garbage into fuel can help the country avoid relying on foreign sources of oil, which has enormous political and economic consequences. David says that turning trash into energy is more reliable than using renewable resources like wind or solar power, safer than using nuclear energy, and more efficient than using food crops like corn or soybeans for energy. For all of these reasons he urges America to look inside its own garbage cans for solutions to energy and environmental problems.

David is a regular contributor to the *Christian Science Monitor*. Mayor George Fitch has just produced a book entitled *A Green Pathway to LOCAL ENERGY INDEPENDENCE*, which identifies exactly how to decentralize energy production and turn municipal waste to local fuel and power.

It's clear that as a major industrial nation America needs to devour enormous amounts of energy to survive. It's also clear America must become energy independent as soon as possible.

Huge amounts of money are spent daily buying energy from foreign nations that have no real respect for our well-being. Permitting America to be dependent on such nations can only lead to complications, especially during times of economic crisis or war.

Like the presidents before him, Barack Obama recognizes the need for US energy independence. In his State of the Union message last week [in January 2010], he recommended that the US seek alternative energy sources and apply innovation to creating clean-energy jobs.

To achieve this end, we mustn't resort to opening more nuclear power plants, as Obama suggested. The United States doesn't need to create radioactive facilities for generating energy. It needs a practical solution to US foreign-oil dependency, one that actually decreases rather than increases waste.

Such a solution is right under our nose. It's one that doesn't depend on high-voltage electric lines; won't reduce the food supply like corn ethanol and soybean diesel; and isn't unreliable like solar, hydro, and wind energy sources.

The solution to our energy independence is in our garbage cans.

Garbage Can Become Fuel

Turning garbage into energy calls to mind the 1980s film "Back to the Future," which inspired whimsical images of future cars powered on waste. Since that time, the technology for turning trash and commercial waste into electricity and biofuel has come a long way. In just the past decade, research and experimentation has brought about a cleaner and more efficient conversion system.

Turning trash and commercial waste into electricity and biofuel has the potential to drastically reduce dependency on foreign oil. It also has the potential to encourage innovation and create jobs.

This plant in Great Britain converts garbage into energy. Turning trash and commercial waste into electricity and biofuel has the potential to drastically reduce dependency on foreign oil, the author claims.

"Trash will move from being a liability to an asset, providing a clean source of energy that can be used where it is produced," alternative IST Energy CEO Stuart Haber recently told ABC News.

Mr. Haber's company is one of the many that has developed equipment to support this statement. His Green Energy Machine, for example, is able to supply sufficient energy for a 200-unit apartment complex with just three tons of trash. During the conversion process, it is capable of eliminating 95 percent of the waste.

A Clean, Efficient Process

Unlike old methods, the new incinerator plants don't require filthy smokestacks that pollute the environment. Instead they create heat in oxygen-starved containers, which turbines or gen-

The United States Lags Behind Europe on Waste to Energy

Many European countries use waste-to-energy plants to keep trash out of landfills and convert it to usable energy. As a result, they have much higher recycling and waste-to-energy rates, and much lower landfilling rates, than the United States.

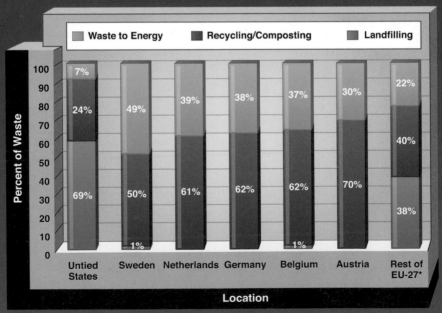

* EU-27: Belgium, Denmark, France, Germany, Greece, Ireland, Italy, Luxembourg, Netherlands, Portugal, Spain, United Kingdom, Austria, Finland, Sweden, Cyprus, Czech Republic, Estonia, Hungary, Latvia, Lithuania, Malta, Poland, Slovakia, Slovenia, Bulgaria, and Romania

Taken from: Shawn Lawrence Otto. *Fool Me Twice: Fighting the Assault on Science in America.* New York: Rodale, 2011.

erators convert into electricity and diesel. As a result, minimum unhealthy emissions are being released into the environment during the conversion process.

Before gasification, waste had no other important usage beyond landfills, which ultimately would contaminate the groundwater with leachates, and produce greenhouse gases.

By converting waste to energy, this contamination is largely avoided and the waste becomes an asset that is capable of supplying communities and large apartment complexes with power.

It is almost perfect.

Unfortunately, not everyone agrees.

Innovation Will Solve Problems

Opponents challenge the cleanliness, the energy efficiency, and even the greenness of thermochemical plants. Their biggest fears are that the production of such waste will create alarming amounts of toxins like dioxin or pollutants like mercury.

But such environmental hazards, when intelligently confronted, can easily be eliminated with new solutions.

The Plasco Energy Group, of Ottawa, Ontario, [Canada,] for example, overcame the dioxin issue by removing all the chlorine before combustion. And the Onondaga County Resource Recovery Agency, of DeWitt, New York, reduced the mercury emission significantly by removing fluorescent lights, batteries, thermostats, and other mercury-laden items from the trash.

Waste to Energy Means a Green, Independent Future

In Warrenton, Va., Mayor George Fitch is hoping to use his town's discarded waste to provide electricity and fuel for its 8,500 residents. By burning 250 tons a day of commercial and residential waste, he believes he will be able to power 60 percent of all the homes and buildings, and provide biofuel for the school buses and public safety vehicles.

With the cooperation of the board of supervisors and a private investment company, he expects the planned thermochemical plant will add to the community's greenness and produce an alternative, forever-renewable energy.

By each of us implementing waste-to-energy projects in our community, together we could significantly make a difference. These projects can be as small as an apartment complex or as large as an entire community.

Our successes can be used as an important model of a sustainable, independent energy program that can be duplicated anywhere in the world. With congressional support and incentives, it will lead to a cleaner and healthier, energy-independent America.

As Mr. Fitch puts it, "Local energy independence is a viable solution to our national energy crisis. We must pursue it and refine it until it works for us perfectly. Failure to move forward now with such an alternative energy plan will only leave America hostage to those foreign interests who would like to control us by gaining a monopoly of our energy supply."

TEN

Trash Should Not Be Recycled into Energy

Global Alliance for Incinerator Alternatives (GAIA)

In the following viewpoint the Global Alliance for Incinerator Alternatives (GAIA) argues that trash should not be recycled into energy. "Waste-to-energy" schemes that burn trash to generate electricity do not actually generate significant amounts of energy—rather, contends GAIA, they make only small amounts of usable energy while destroying other useful materials. GAIA also blames the incineration process for releasing toxic pollutants and contributing to climate change. Furthermore, burning garbage is much more expensive than creating other forms of energy, and takes resources and attention away from more environmentally friendly waste solutions, such as composting and recycling, the organization maintains. For all of these reasons, GAIA concludes that recycling trash into energy wastes money and causes pollution.

GAIA is a nonprofit organization that opposes the use of incinerators on the grounds that they pollute the environment.

Incineration is a waste treatment technology that involves burning commercial, residential and hazardous waste. Incineration converts discarded materials, including paper, plastics, metals and food scraps into bottom ash, fly ash, combustion gases, air pollutants, wastewater, wastewater treatment sludge and heat. There are 113 waste incinerators in the U.S. and 86 of these are used to generate electricity. No new incinerators have been built in the U.S. after 1997, due to public opposition, identified health risks, high costs, and the increase of practices such as recycling and composting. In recent years, the incinerator industry has tried to expand their sector by marketing their facilities as "Waste to Energy" (WTE), using misleading claims.

Not a Source of Renewable Energy

Municipal waste is non-renewable, consisting of discarded materials such as paper, plastic and glass that are derived from finite natural resources such as forests that are being depleted at unsustainable rates. Burning these materials in order to generate electricity creates a demand for "waste" and discourages much-needed efforts to conserve resources, reduce packaging and waste and encourage recycling and composting. More than 90% of materials currently disposed of in incinerators and landfills can be reused, recycled and composted. Providing subsidies or incentives for incineration encourages local governments to destroy these materials, rather than investing in environmentally sound and energy conserving practices such as recycling and composting.

Adding to the Pollution Problem

All incinerators pose considerable risk to the health and environment of neighboring communities as well as that of the general population. Even the most technologically advanced incinerators release thousands of pollutants that contaminate our air, soil and water. Many of these pollutants enter the food supply and concentrate up through the food chain. Incinerator workers and people living near incinerators are particularly at high risk of exposure to dioxin and other contaminants. A recent [2011] study published in the *American Economic Review* found that among U.S. industries, the waste incineration industry has the highest ratio of negative economic impacts from air pollution compared to the financial value added by the industry.

The New York Department of Conservation found that the state's incinerators emit up to 14 times more mercury as coal-fired power plants per unit of energy. In 2009, New York incinerators emitted a total of 36% more mercury than its coal plants.

In newer incinerators, air pollution control devices such as air filters capture and concentrate some of the pollutants; but they don't eliminate them. The captured pollutants are transferred to other by-products such as fly ash, bottom ash, boiler ash/slag, and wastewater treatment sludge that are then released into the environment. However, even modern pollution control devices such as air filters do not prevent the escape of many hazardous emissions such as ultra-fine particles. Ultra-fine particles are particles produced from burning materials (including PCBs, dioxins and furans), which are smaller in size than what is currently regulated or monitored by the U.S. EPA [Environmental Protection Agency]. These particles can be lethal, causing cancer, heart attacks, strokes, asthma, and pulmonary disease. It is estimated that airborne particulates cause the deaths of over 2 million people worldwide each year. In the U.S. communities of color, low-income communities, and indigenous communities are exposed to a disproportionate burden of such toxins.

Finally, U.S. regulatory agencies have found that incinerators are prone to various types of malfunctions, system failures and breakdowns, which routinely lead to serious air pollution control problems and increased emissions that are dangerous to public health.

Burning Waste Contributes to Climate Change

Incinerators emit more carbon dioxide (CO_2) per unit of electricity (2988 lbs/MWh [megawatt hour]) than coal-fired power plants (2249 lbs/MWh). According to the U.S. EPA, "waste to energy" incinerators and landfills contribute far higher levels of greenhouse gas emissions and overall energy throughout their lifecycles

Waste-to-Energy Plants Create Pollution

Air Emissions:
Landfill Scenario vs. Waste-to-Energy (WTE) Scenario

Waste-to-energy facilities release fewer air pollutants than landfills but release much higher levels of heavy metals such as mercury, cadmium, and lead.

Parameter	Unit	Landfill Scenario	WTE Scenario
Nitrogen Oxides	g/tonne[1] of MSW[2]	470	190
Sulphur Oxides	g/tonne of MSW	56	84
Carbon Monoxide	g/tonne of MSW	6,100	90
Particulate Matter	g/tonne of MSW	13	3
Mercury	mg/tonne[3] of MSW	0.347	31.9
Cadmium	mg/tonne of MSW	-0.024	4.11
Lead	mg/tonne of MSW	6.46	48.56
Dioxins	g/tonne of MSW	.019	.032

1. gram/tonne (g/tonne)   2. municipal solid waste (MSW)   3. milligram/tonne (mg/tonne)

Taken from: The Sheltair Group. *Environmental Life Cycle Assessment of Solid Waste Management: Evaluation of Two Waste Disposal Scenarios for the Metro Vancouver Region, 2008; Jordan Best, Examining the Waste–to–Energy Option,* Recycling Council of British Columbia, 2008.

than source reduction, reuse and recycling of the same materials. Incineration also drives a climate changing cycle of new resources pulled out of the earth, processed in factories, shipped around the world, and then wasted in incinerators and landfills.

Denmark—the poster child of Europe's incinerator industry—recently discovered that its incinerators were releasing double the quantity of carbon dioxide than originally estimated, and had probably been doing so for years, causing Denmark to miss its Kyoto Protocol GHG [greenhouse gas] reduction targets.

In contrast, a 2009 study by the EPA concluded that up to 42% of U.S. GHG emissions could be impacted through zero waste strategies such as recycling and composting.

A Massive Waste of Energy and a Poor Source of Jobs

Due to the low calorific [energy] value of waste, incinerators are only able to make small amounts of energy while destroying large amounts of reusable materials. While older incinerators generate electricity at very low efficiency rates of 19–27%, a recent UK [United Kingdom] study found that conversion efficiencies of new incineration technologies are even lower. Conversely, zero waste practices such as recycling and composting serve to conserve three to five times the amount of energy produced by waste incineration. The amount of energy wasted in the U.S. by not recycling aluminum and steel cans, paper, printed materials, glass, and plastic is equal to the annual output of 15 medium-sized power plants.

Recycling creates 10–20 times more jobs than incinerators. Incinerators require huge capital investment, but they offer relatively few jobs when compared to recycling. With a national recycling rate of less than 33%, the U.S. recycling industries currently provide over 800,000 jobs. A national recycling rate of 75% would create 1.5 million jobs.

A Waste of Money

Incinerators are the most expensive method to generate energy and to handle waste, while also creating significant economic burdens for host cities. According to the U.S. Energy Information Administration Annual Energy Outlook 2010, the projected capital cost of new waste incinerator facilities is $8,232 per kilowatt hour. That is twice the cost of coal-fired power and 60 percent more than nuclear energy. Waste incinerator operations and maintenance costs are ten times greater than coal and four times greater than nuclear.

Billions of taxpayer dollars are spent subsidizing the construction and operations of incinerators. In 2011, Harrisburg, PA became the largest U.S. city to declare bankruptcy, and the financial blame rests squarely on the shoulders of its staggering debt payments for upgrades at the city's incinerator. Detroit taxpayers have spent over $1.2 billion dollars in debt service payments from constructing and upgrading the world's largest waste incinerator. As a result, residents have had to pay high trash disposal fees of over $150 per ton. The city could have saved over $55 million in just one year if it had never built the incinerator. For a fraction of these costs, investments in recycling, reuse and remanufacturing would create significantly more business and employment opportunities.

Taking Away from More-Effective Programs

Fact: Incinerators burn many valuable resources that can be recycled and composted, and incinerators compete for the same materials as recycling programs. Because of the extremely high costs of constructing and operating an incinerator, spending taxpayer money for an incinerator means that there are significantly less funds to invest in more affordable solutions. More than two thirds of the materials we use are still burned or buried, despite the fact that we can cost-effectively recycle the vast majority of what we waste.

Countries and regions in Europe that have high waste incineration rates typically recycle less. Data for household waste from Denmark in 2005 clearly shows that regions with expanded incineration have lower recycling and regions with lower incineration do more recycling. It's worth noting that Denmark's recycling rate is well behind other regions of Europe such as Flanders in Belgium, which recycles 71% of municipal waste.

According to Eurostat in 2007, Denmark generates some of the highest per capita waste in the EU [European Union] (over 1762 lbs. each year) and over 80% of what is burned in Danish incinerators is recyclable and compostable. A 2009 study reported that Europe throws away resources worth over $6 billion dollars every year by burning and burying materials that can be recycled.

This garbage incineration plant in the UK turns discarded materials, including paper, plastics, metals, and food scraps, into a different sort of trash, such as bottom ash, fly ash, combustion gases, air pollutants, wastewater, and wastewater treatment sludge, which is why the author disapproves of such incineration.

Adding to the Problem

Waste incinerators in the EU continue to pollute the climate and cause significant public health risk, while burning billions of dollars-worth of valuable, non-renewable resources. A recent public health impacts report states that modern incinerators in the EU are a major source of ultra-fine particulate emissions. In 2009, the Advertising Standards Agency in the UK banned the SITA Cornwall waste company from distributing its booklet on incineration for, among other things, making unsubstantiated claims that the UK Health Protection Agency stated that modern incinerators are safe.

ELEVEN

Electronics Recycling Does Not Pollute Third World Countries

Adam Minter

> The vast majority of electronic waste, or e-waste, from the United States is not irresponsibly dumped overseas, argues Adam Minter in the following viewpoint. Minter contends that fears about recycled electronics ending up in vast, polluting dumping grounds are unfounded because most recycled electronics are processed domestically in the United States. The electronics that are sent abroad are typically not even dismantled, according to Minter. Rather, they are kept whole and used by people or companies that are unable to afford brand-new cell phones, computers, video game consoles, or printers. Minter laments that hysteria over a "toxic tide" of overseas e-waste has kept some consumers from recycling their old electronics. He maintains that the majority of recycled e-waste is neither dumped overseas nor handled irresponsibly.
>
> Minter is the Shanghai, China, correspondent for the *World View* blog at Bloomberg, a business website. He is also the author of the book *Junkyard Planet*.

Every year, Americans toss out as much as 4.5 million tons of old mobile phones, laptops, televisions, Xboxes and other electronic gadgets.

Some is recycled; some is repaired and refurbished for reuse; and some is thrown into landfills or incinerators. Almost none of it, however, is "dumped" overseas.

Most E-Waste Is Recycled Domestically

That, at least, is the conclusion of the first comprehensive survey of what happens to U.S. e-waste [electronic waste] after it is dropped into a recycling bin. Published in February [2013], the study by the U.S. International Trade Commission surveyed 5,200 businesses involved in the e-waste industry (companies that received the survey were required by law to complete it, and to do so accurately), and found that almost 83 percent of what was put into American recycling bins in 2011 was repaired, dismantled or recycled domestically.

According to the same survey, only 0.13 percent of the 4.4 million tons of e-waste that Americans generated in 2011 was sent overseas for "final disposal"—a term that explicitly excludes recycling and reuse—with an additional 3 percent sent abroad for "unknown" purposes.

Reality is a far cry from the long-standing claim, first made by the Basel Action Network, a Seattle [Washington]–based nongovernmental organization in 2002, that as much as 80 percent of U.S. e-waste is exported to the developing world. Amazingly, even with the wide currency the claim has enjoyed over the years among environmental organizations and the media, it was never based on a systematic study.

Exported E-Waste Helps Bridge the Digital Gap

This misunderstanding has led to several efforts at erecting partial export bans on U.S. electronics to developing countries, which—other studies demonstrate—import them as cheap and sustainable alternatives to new equipment. As a result, perfectly usable electronics are diverted into a recycling stream, where they are turned into raw materials, rather than into markets where they can be reused for years.

A worker disassembles an old TV at a recycling plant in China. American e-waste was used by the Chinese from the 1990s through the early 2000s to help them bridge the digital gap.

There are no statistics on how many used gadgets were exported from the U.S. to the developing world in 2002. Nor, for that matter, can anyone say for sure what happened to those gadgets. No doubt, many were broken down in developing-world facilities, where low-technology and often-hazardous methods of recycling and disposal were employed (such as the use of acids to strip copper and other metals from circuit boards in open, unprotected environments).

Anecdotally, I have been told by recyclers in southern China that cheap, secondhand electronics exported from the U.S. and, to a lesser extent, the European Union [EU] were used by Chinese computer labs, offices and dormitories in the 1990s through the mid-2000s, when new gadgetry simply wasn't affordable. (There has been no comprehensive survey to verify these claims, however.)

It was a good deal for the U.S., too: In the 1990s and early 2000s, America didn't really have an electronics-recycling sector, and those machines would have been put in a landfill if China hadn't wanted them. Nonetheless, as China developed, and incomes rose, demand for those used machines dropped off.

The good news is that a similar cycle is occurring in Africa, where used electronics from the EU and the U.S. have become a critical means of bridging the global digital gap. Unlike Chinese imports in the 1990s and early 2000s, the African imports are being surveyed and quantified.

Most Recycled Electronics Are Used by People Who Need Them

For example, a 2011 study by the United Nations Environment Program determined that only 9 percent of the used electronics imported by Nigeria—a country that is regularly depicted as a dumping ground for foreign e-waste—didn't work or were unrepairable, and thus bound for a recycler or a dump. The other 91 percent were reusable and bound for consumers who couldn't afford new products.

That certainly doesn't excuse the hazardous means that some Nigerians use to recycle old electronics (and, increasingly, those old electronics are thrown away by middle-class Nigerians, rather than being imported from abroad). Yet it also doesn't suggest that the U.S., Europe or even China (a growing source of e-waste) are to blame, either.

So what happens to the 14 percent of U.S. e-waste that isn't processed domestically, sent for "final disposal" in other countries, or isn't otherwise unknown? According to the trade commission report, most is exported as recycled commodities to be reused by manufacturers in new products; as reusable gadgets; and even as warrantied products for repair.

Less than half of those exports, by weight, go to developing countries; the majority is shipped to member countries of the Organization for Economic Co-operation and Development, such as Japan and Belgium, where the recyclable material is handled better in factories than it can be in America.

Exported E-Waste Is Usually Handled Responsibly

The U.S. shipped almost three times as much e-waste to Belgium in 2011 as it did to sub-Saharan Africa, according to the trade commission.

Why? Belgium has one of the world's best (and cleanest) factories for the extraction of precious metals from circuit boards and other complicated devices. It is thus capable of paying far more for them than a recycler in Nigeria with little more than some jars of acid capable of refining gold, though not platinum and other precious metals.

The biggest story embedded in the trade commission's story isn't that U.S. e-waste exports are greener than ever. Rather it is that the domestic electronics-recycling industry has grown into a large, mature business that views export as a second choice, not the first one.

The industry generated sales of $20.6 billion in 2011, compared with less than $1 billion in 2002, according to figures from the trade commission as well as the Institute of Scrap Recycling Industries, an industry association.

The Myth of the "Toxic Tide"

E-Stewards, a strict, U.S.-based electronics recycling certification standard that bans most exports, has grown from having zero member facilities certified in 2010 to 102 in 2013, including several belonging to Waste Management, North America's largest recycling company. Most of what these companies—certified or not—produce are commodity-grade raw materials, such as metals and plastics, usable for new products in the U.S. and abroad.

A February 2013 report by the United States International Trade Commission found that the vast majority of used electronic products (UEPs) stay in the United States. The UEPs that are exported abroad are largely resold as intact products intended for reuse.

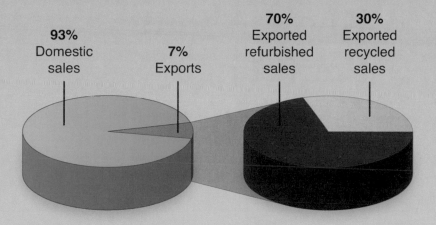

93% Domestic sales   **7%** Exports   **70%** Exported refurbished sales   **30%** Exported recycled sales

Total = $19.4 billion dollars   **Total = $1.5 billion dollars**

Taken from: United States International Trade Commission. "Used Electronic Products: An Examination of US Exports." USITC Publication no. 4379, February 2013.

More revealing, yet, is the employment picture: The institute estimates full-time jobs in the U.S. electronics-recycling industry grew to more than 45,000 in 2011 from 6,000 in 2002. Some of those employees, no doubt, are involved in packing used electronics for shipment around the world, including to places where unsafe, environmentally damaging means of disposal are still used.

Thanks to the International Trade Commission findings and other, smaller-scale studies, we now know that most secondhand electronics are reused and recycled in the U.S. The toxic tide that frightened Americans into stashing their old computers in closets turns out to be nothing more threatening than a trickle.

What You Should Know About Recycling

Facts About Trash in the United States
According to Edward Humes in *Garbology: Our Dirty Love Affair with Trash*, every American will throw away 102 tons of garbage in a lifetime.

Waste Management (WM) Recycle America asserts that
- over a lifetime the average American disposes of garbage that totals six hundred times his or her adult weight;
- each year Americans dispose of so much office paper that it could build a wall twelve feet high from Los Angeles to New York City;
- the entire US commercial air fleet could be rebuilt using the amount of aluminum thrown away by the nation every three months.

According to the 2010 report *Recycling Myths Revisited* by the Property and Environment Research Center (PERC),
- in 1987 the garbage barge *Mobro* traveled six thousand miles down the Atlantic seaboard from New York to the Gulf of Mexico looking for a place to dump its cargo of thirty-two hundred tons of trash;
- if a landfill's trash were piled 255 feet high, it would hold all of the nation's garbage for the next hundred years in a space of about ten square miles;

- in the late 1970s and 1980s the amount of plastic packaging thrown into landfills increased, yet its total weight dropped by 40 percent, which was due to lighter-weight packaging that has reduced the weight of two-liter soda bottles by 30 percent and plastic bags by 70 percent;
- the *Oregonian* newspaper of Portland, Oregon, once claimed that disposable diapers composed 25 percent of the area's landfills, but further research concluded that they account for only about 1 percent of trash.

Facts About Recycling in the United States

According to a 2011 poll by Ipsos Public Affairs, the most common items recycled by Americans are:
- plastic, as in beverage bottles and packaging (69 percent);
- metal, including soda and soup cans (64 percent);
- newspaper (56 percent);
- other paper, such as cardboard and magazines (56 percent);
- glass jars and bottles (49 percent);
- electronics, such as CDs or computer parts, (14 percent).

According to WM Recycle America,
  recycling benefits the environment because it
    - spares natural resources,
    - conserves energy,
    - conserves clean air and water,
    - saves landfill space;
most paper can be recycled several times by using the following process:
    - Recycled paper is collected, sorted, baled, and taken to a paper mill;
    - a hydrapulper, resembling a giant blender, mixes water with the paper, separates inks from the paper fibers, and pulls the fibers apart;
    - the pulp filters through screens that catch contaminants, including paper clips and staples;
    - new wood pulp is usually mixed in, which strengthens the paper; and finally,
    - it is formed into sheets, dried, finished, and rolled.

PERC asserts the following in *Recycling Mythis Revisited*:

- Neighborhood recycling pickup requires its own fleet of trucks. The city of Los Angeles estimates that its curbside recycling program doubled its number of trucks from four hundred to eight hundred. More trucks require more iron ore, steel, rubber, and petroleum, and produce more air-polluting exhaust.
- Some clothing makers never recovered from the federal Wool Products Labeling Act of 1939, which mandated the labeling of items made from recycled wool and cotton; consumers assumed such products were inferior and avoided them.
- Every year the Institute of Scrap Recycling Industries recycles 96 million tons of metals and 54 million tons of paper, glass, and plastic. This far surpasses the amount collected by all city, county, and state residential programs.

Facts About Resources Saved by Recycling
According to the town of New Canaan, Connecticut,

- making recycled paper uses 30 to 55 percent less energy than making it from scratch;
- someone who recycles a foot-high stack of newspaper conserves enough energy to take a hot shower each day for a week;
- to recycle 150 pounds of paper spares one tree and yields 95 percent less air pollution;
- every ton of newspaper recycled conserves seventeen trees and an amount of energy equal to one hundred gallons of gasoline;
- anyone who recycles a newspaper every day for a year saves five trees;
- manufacturing a three-subject notebook from recycled paper (instead of from new paper) uses ten fewer gallons of water and releases 2.1 fewer pounds of carbon dioxide into the atmosphere;
- making recycled plastic uses 88 percent less energy than making new plastic;

- all plastic contains petroleum, a nonrenewable resource that could be used to power cars or buses;
- recycling one plastic bottle saves enough energy to run a computer for twenty-five minutes;
- the plastic in five bottles can be broken down into enough polyester fiber to make one square foot of carpet, an extra large T-shirt, or the filling for a ski jacket, whereas two bottles are enough to produce the polyester for one baseball cap;
- annually, the average household discards about eighty-eight pounds of plastic;
- a park bench made of recycled plastic holds the equivalent of about a thousand bottles and milk jugs;
- each ton of aluminum recycled saves the same amount of energy contained in 2,350 gallons of gasoline;
- recycling one aluminum can requires the amount of energy equal to that of only a tablespoon of gasoline;
- making recycled glass produces 20 percent less air pollution and half as much water pollution as does making new glass;
- every glass bottle that is recycled conserves enough energy to power a hundred-watt bulb for 4 hours or a TV for 1.5 hours;
- recycling creates jobs because for every ten thousand tons of plastic, burning it creates one job, shipping it to landfills creates six jobs, and recycling it requires thirty-six jobs.

American Opinions About Recycling

A national survey by Ipsos Public Affairs in 2011 found that
- among American adults, 87 percent recycle, of which about half recycle every day and 36 percent do so less often, while 13 percent never recycle;
- people most likely to recycle every day are college graduates, fifty-five years or older, and living in the Northeast and the West;
- when asked about the advantages of recycling, 81 percent say it saves space in landfills, 69 percent report that it conserves trees, 62 percent say it saves energy, 45 percent think it creates jobs, and 33 percent believe that it raises money, whereas only 3 percent are unsure or do not believe it has benefits;

the reasons people give for not recycling more include: It is not accessible or convenient where they live (25 percent), it takes too much time (10 percent), they forget (10 percent), they are not sure what is and is not recyclable (8 percent), it costs too much (6 percent);

- 46 percent of people use curbside recycling, 26 percent drop off materials at a local center, and 6 percent recycle mostly at work;
- 78 percent of people are aware that cell phones can be recycled, while 67 percent know motor oil can be recycled;
- only 36 percent know that less common items, such as trophies and crayons, are recyclable; and
- more than 70 percent of people erroneously think that pizza boxes and juice boxes can be recycled, though waxy paper and contaminated cardboard are not recyclable.

What You Should Do About Recycling

According to the Environmental Protection Agency (EPA), each day every American throws away about 4.5 pounds of garbage, a big increase from 2.7 pounds in 1960. This amounts to sixty-three thousand full garbage trucks per day in the United States alone. As more Americans create more and more garbage, society has grappled with how to handle the additional waste and has often come back to recycling as an answer. About 75 percent of trash is recyclable, yet only about 30 percent is recycled, according to the EPA. You can increase the amount of waste that gets recycled by buying (and encouraging your family to buy) notebooks made from recycled paper; drinks that come in recycled glass bottles; and school supplies, toys, bags, and other products made from recycled plastic, as well as by recycling items after you have used them.

The Importance of Recycling

As you learned from reading the viewpoints in this book, there is debate over whether recycling is environmentally friendly or saves or wastes resources. Although many people argue there is plenty of room in landfills and that recycling does not save resources, many others worry that without recycling, the planet's valuable resources will be squandered at too fast a rate. For example, according to GreenWaste recycling service, the amount of wood and paper that goes unrecycled each year would be enough to heat 50 million homes for twenty years. Also, the world's supply of oil—a necessity in manufacturing plastic and other materials—is dwindling. The International Energy Agency warns that oil and gas production will drop 40–60 percent by 2030. Making new products uses a lot of oil and pollutes water and air. Therefore, proponents of recycling argue that the process requires fewer resources, pollutes less, and saves room in landfills.

If you have come to the opinion that recycling is inefficient and wastes resources, the best thing for you to do about it is put together an informed campaign that explores which types of recycling are most beneficial, and what alternative methods can be taken (such as reducing the initial amount of waste or reusing items). If you support recycling, you can take numerous steps to encourage or improve recycling programs in your home or school.

Recycling at Home

If your household does not recycle, find out why. Perhaps family members hold strong views about recycling: They may think it is a waste of time, a dirty hassle, or remain otherwise unconvinced of its environmental benefits. If this is the case, hold an informal debate about the merits and drawbacks of recycling. Have each family member research a position and present it to the others.

Perhaps your family wants to recycle but does not do so because they are unaware of recycling programs in your area. They probably need not look far: A study by Moore Recycling found that over 70 percent of Americans have recycling bins for plastics within ten miles of their homes. Grocery stores now collect plastic bags for recycling. In addition, there are over nine thousand curbside pickup programs across the country, according to Earth911, an online resource of environmental information. You can find out whether you have this service by calling or checking the website of your local recycling, transportation, or sanitation department. It can provide details about what types of materials can be recycled, how to sort them, and when and where you need to leave them.

If you do not have curbside pickup, recycling may be more challenging, but it is still doable. Look up the location and hours of nearby recycling centers and set a day and time when you can help your family drop off recyclables. Teenager Shana Cameron explains how she took charge of recycling in her family: "We drink tons and tons of milk at my house every week, probably seven gallons a week. . . . My parents don't like [the empty jugs] sitting around the house, so I throw them in the trunk of my car, and when I can't fit anything else in my trunk, I drive to Kroger [supermarket], which is right by my house, and they have the big recycling bins over there."[1] It also helps to know whether your state offers a cash refund for cans, plastic drink bottles, and glass. Money can be a good incentive for your family to recycle, especially if you decide together how you plan to spend the proceeds earned from it.

If your household is in agreement about recycling, make sure all members know what materials are recyclable. Designate a place for recyclables in or outside your home, and know your city's requirements for sorting them. In many places, plastic bottles need to be separated by number (which appears on the bottom) and glass by color. Also help your family remember by writing on a calendar and reminding them what days the recyclables need to be ready for pickup or drop-off.

If your family remains unconvinced about recycling, there are actions you can take on your own. Look for other uses for disposables rather than discarding them. You can wash out glass jelly or spaghetti sauce jars and use them for unique crafts projects, such as making candleholders, dessert bowls, screw and nail organizers, and other useful items. Numerous decorations and art projects can also be fashioned out of aluminum, cardboard, and other materials— check websites like Pinterest for an almost endless array of creative ideas. Several other websites teach young people how to start their own compost pile to recycle food scraps and grow a garden. There are also sites that offer step-by-step guides to teach beginners how to fix broken mp3 players, game consoles, and DVD players, which keeps these items from entering landfills and saves you money. Another option is to see whether your school will allow you to bring recyclables from home and put them in the school's bins.

Recycling at School

Up to 80 percent of school waste is recyclable, which has prompted many districts to start recycling programs. If your school does not have one, find out why. Is it too expensive? Does it violate some kind of permit restriction? Launch an investigation into why your school lacks such a program and investigate what it would take to start one.

If your school does have a recycling program, ask the teacher in charge how you can help. Perhaps they need students to pick up recyclables from the drop boxes, sort materials, remove bottle caps that cannot be recycled, or crush plastic bottles flat to save space. Each teacher should have a recycling bin or know where to take recyclables, and students should know, too. You may be asked to spread the word about the program by hanging posters around school, making announcements over the intercom, or writing an article for your school's newsletter, newspaper, or blog.

Some schools recycle only paper. See whether you can help expand your school's program to include as many types of materials as possible. If your school does not have a system in place for recycling old electronics, perhaps you can start one. The Consumer Electronics Association notes that the average household has twenty-four recyclable electronic devices that are often thrown away when family members upgrade to a newer model. Instead, your school can donate working electronics to the needy. Broken computers, used batteries, empty print cartridges, and other electronic waste can be recycled at certain retail stores for free. Cell phones are not only recyclable but may earn cash. Some organizations sponsor cell phone drives and will send your school prepaid shipping labels as well as money in return for each phone.

No matter how you incorporate recycling into your home, school, or community, make sure you use the resources in this book to arm yourself with information about the process so you can speak knowledgably about whatever course of action you choose to pursue.

Notes
1. Moira Corcoran, "Recycling, One Milk Carton at a Time," What Kids Can Do, June 2009. www.whatkidscando.org.

ORGANIZATIONS TO CONTACT

The editors have compiled the following list of organizations concerned with the issues debated in this book. The descriptions are derived from materials provided by the organizations. All have publications or information available for interested readers. The list was compiled on the date of publication of the present volume; names, addresses, phone and fax numbers, and e-mail and Internet addresses may change. Be aware that many organizations take several weeks or longer to respond to inquiries, so allow as much time as possible.

American Chemistry Council (ACC), Plastics Division
700 Second St. NE, Washington, DC 20002
(202) 249-7000
website: http://plastics.americanchemistry.com

The ACC is a trade association that represents chemists. Its Plastics Division works to develop lighter-weight plastics, promote plastics recycling, and encourage the expansion of neighborhood recycling programs. Its website has statistics on plastic manufacturing, videos on how to recycle plastics, a wealth of information on plastic bottle and bag recycling, and various reports and brochures, including "Take a Closer Look at Today's Polystyrene Packaging—Safe, Affordable, and Environmentally Responsible."

Basel Action Network (BAN)
206 First Ave. South, Ste. 410, Seattle, WA 98104
(206) 652-5555
e-mail: inform@ban.org
website: www.ban.org

BAN's aim is to prevent the export of toxic products, waste, and technologies from industrialized nations to poorer ones, as well as to promote sustainable waste practices. It campaigns against electronic waste (e-waste), conducts research, and works with countries to set environmentally responsible policy. Toward its goal to disseminate information on all issues pertaining to toxic trade, BAN produces an e-newsletter, articles in research journals, and video documentaries.

Global Alliance for Incinerator Alternatives/Global Anti-Incinerator Alliance (GAIA)
1958 University Ave., Berkeley, CA 94704
(510) 883-9490
website: www.no-burn.org

GAIA is an alliance of groups and individuals from almost a hundred countries who work toward creating a toxin-free planet without incinerators or polluting technologies. It also promotes environmental justice, local green economies, and zero-waste living. On its website are case studies, fact sheets, its bimonthly newsletter, and GAIA publications such as *On the Road to Zero Waste: Successes and Lessons from Around the World* and *Respect for Recyclers: Protecting the Climate Through Zero Waste*.

GrassRoots Recycling Network
672 Robinson Rd., Sebastopol, CA 95472
website: www.grrn.org

This organization calls for the world's citizens to go beyond recycling by living lifestyles that produce zero waste. Its goal is for all manufacturers to produce nontoxic items designed to be recovered for reuse, recycling, or composting, with no trash to be burned or buried. Visitors to the website can join the e-mail listserve and GreenYes and download the Zero Waste Briefing Kit, which includes case studies, charts, and statistics.

Institute for Local Self Reliance (ILSR)
2001 S St. NW, Ste. 570, Washington, DC 20009
(202) 898-1610
website: www.ilsr.org

ILSR empowers communities to be self-sufficient in meeting their own local and regional needs, because it believes federal policy does not protect the interests of, and often harms, cities and communities. Its Waste to Wealth initiative focuses on reducing waste through education, legislation, and political activism. Numerous news articles and reports are available on its website.

National Center for Electronics Recycling (NCER)
115 Rosemar Rd., Ste. 2, Parkersburg, WV 26104
website: www.electronicsrecycling.org

NCER is a nonprofit group that advocates national programs to encourage recycling of electronics. It provides a directory of electronics recyclers, a map with state laws pertaining to e-waste and recycling, and best practices for manufacturers. Its website also makes available news releases, archived issues of its e-newsletter, and testimony of congressional hearings on electronics recycling.

Stop Waste
1537 Webster St., Oakland, CA 94612
(510) 891-6500
website: www.stopwaste.org

Although the Stop Waste program is run by the Alameda County (California) Waste Management Authority and the Alameda County Source Reduction and Recycling Board, it offers a wealth of resources useful to citizens across the nation. It provides news, success stories, and starter kits with posters and decals for those new to recycling and also publishes advice on recycling, reducing waste, and shopping green.

US Environmental Protection Agency (EPA)
1200 Pennsylvania Ave. NW, Washington, DC 20460
(202) 272-0167
website: www.epa.gov/students

The EPA is the US government agency charged with protecting citizens' health at home, school, and the workplace, as well as maintaining the health of the environment. It writes and enforces legislation to this end. Its website's section for students includes games, quizzes, ideas for science fair projects, and resources to help with homework.

Waste Management (WM) Recycle America
1001 Fannin St., Ste. 4000, Houston, TX 77002
(713) 512-6200
website: www.recycleamerica.com

As an operator of nearly a hundred recycling facilities, one plastics recycling plant, and three electronics recycling facilities, WM Recycle America offers waste management information and solutions for households, businesses, and manufacturers. The "Press Room" page of its website contains current and archived news, and its Educational Resources section is useful for children, students, teachers, and researchers.

BIBLIOGRAPHY

Books

Catherine Alexander and Joshua Reno, eds., *Economies of Recycling: Global Transformations of Materials, Values and Social Relations*. London: Zed Books, 2012. This anthology investigates how products are manufactured and their waste shipped around the globe. It profiles workers in the garbage industry and case studies across Europe, Asia, Africa, and the Americas.

Russel Gehrke, *Recycling Projects for the Evil Genius*. New York: McGraw-Hill/TAB Electronics, 2010. An introduction to main concepts behind recycling and a guide to do-it-yourself, environmentally friendly projects, which may require an adult's help. Readers can make papier-mâché objects from waste paper, a pet bed from plastic grocery bags, and oil candles from glass bottles and then sell their creations.

Richard Heinberg and Daniel Lerch, eds., *The Post Carbon Reader: Managing the 21st Century's Sustainability Crises*. Healdsburg, CA: Watershed Media, 2010. Winner of the gold medal from the Independent Publisher Book Awards in Environment/Ecology/ Nature, this anthology covers waste, depletion of oil and other resources, climate change, renewable energy, nuclear power, and urban farming.

Edward Humes, *Garbology: Our Dirty Love Affair with Trash*. New York: Avery, 2012. A Pulitzer Prize–winning author delves into all aspects of trash in a quest to solve the problem of waste in the United States. He discusses reusable shopping bags, feeding garbage to pigs, and no-trash lifestyles, among other strategies.

Samantha MacBride, *Recycling Reconsidered: The Present Failure and Future Promise of Environmental Action in the United States*. Cambridge, MA: MIT Press, 2011. A former deputy director for recycling at New York's Department of Sanitation critically examines the recycling movement in America. She argues that a singular focus on recycling has stalled efforts to implement more-sustainable practices of reducing garbage.

Jacqueline Vaughn, *Waste Management: A Reference Handbook*. Santa Barbara, CA: ABC-CLIO, 2009. In this comprehensive source, professor and environmentalist Vaughn covers an array of topics, including history, controversies, new developments, and global issues of refuse and recycling.

Periodicals and Internet Sources

Rick Badie, "Recycling Tires Saves Money, Creates Jobs," *Atlanta Forward* (blog), August 1, 2012. http://blogs.ajc.com/atlanta -forward/2012/08/01/recycling-tires-saves-money-creates-jobs.

Elizabeth Balkan, "The Dirty Truth About China's Incinerators," *Guardian* (Manchester, UK), July 4, 2012. www.theguardian .com/environment/2012/jul/04/dirty-truth-chinas-incinerators.

Daniel K. Benjamin, *Recycling Myths Revisited*, PERC Policy Series no. 47, Property and Environment Research Center, 2010. http://perc.org/sites/default/files/ps47.pdf.

David Biello, "Trashed Tech Dumped Overseas: Does the U.S. Care?," *Scientific American*, September 19, 2008.

Sabrina Bornstein, "Throwing Away Jobs: How More Recycling Could Boost the Economy," Frying Pan News, November 21, 2011. http://fryingpannews.org/2011/11/21/throwing-away-jobs -how-more-recycling-could-boost-the-economy.

Susan Burton, "Recycling? Fuhgeddaboudit," *Mother Jones*, May /June 2009.

Per Bylund, "The Recycling Myth," *Mises Daily*, Ludwig von Mises Institute, February 4, 2008. http://mises.org/daily/2855.

Cristen Conger, "Is Recycling Worth It?," *Discovery News*, December 28, 2010. http://news.discovery.com/tech/is-recycling -worth-it.htm.

County of Santa Barbara Resource Recovery & Waste Management Division, "Why Recycle?," 2013. www.lessismore.org. /materials/28-why-recycle?fromsearch=Why%20Recycle?

John P. DeVillars, "It's Not Waste; It's Energy," *Boston Globe*, December 2, 2009.

Florida Sierra Club, "Recycling Versus Waste to Energy." http:// florida.sierraclub.org/posdocs/Recycl_vs_Waste_to_Energy .pdf.

Jessica Garrison, "Recycling Fraud Is Draining California Cash," *Los Angeles Times*, October 7, 2012.

Erica Gies, "When Trash Becomes a Resource," *Forbes*, February 29, 2012.

Jay Hancock, "Waste-to-Energy Plant Could Be Model for Maryland's Electric Future," *Baltimore Sun*, September 10, 2011.

Carolyn D. Heising, "Recycling Nuclear Waste Makes Sense for Energy Future," *Cedar Rapids (IA) Gazette*, October 26, 2011. http://thegazette.com/2011/10/26/recycling-nuclear-waste -makes-sense-for-energy-future.

Jeff Jacoby, "Get Excited About Recycling? Not Me," *Boston Globe*, September 19, 2010.

———, "The Waste of Recycling," *Boston Globe*, September 22, 2010.

Matt Kasper, "Energy from Waste Can Help Curb Greenhouse Gas Emissions," Center for American Progress, April 17, 2013. www .americanprogress.org/issues/green/report/2013/04/17/60712 /energy-from-waste-can-help-curb-greenhouse-gas-emissions.

Martin LaMonica, "Waste to Energy: Green or Greenwash?," CNET, October 21, 2011. http://news.cnet.com/8301-11128_3 -20123706-54/waste-to-energy-green-or-greenwash.

Steve Larkin, "Private Sector 'Green Jobs' Trump Federally Subsidized Ones," Cleveland.com, June 18, 2011. www.cleve land.com/opinion/index.ssf/2011/06/private_sector_green_jobs _trum.html.

Iain Murray, "Time to Recycle Recycling?," Competitive Enterprise Institute, June 16, 2008. http://cei.org/op-eds-and-articles/time -recycle-recycling.

Brendan O'Neill, "Sorting Rubbish into Different Bins Is Nothing More than a Useless Religious Ritual Forced on Us by the Green Lobby," *Telegraph* (London), February 17, 2011. http://blogs.tele graph.co.uk/news/brendanoneill2/100076651/sorting-rubbish -into-different-bins-is-nothing-more-than-a-useless-religious -ritual-forced-on-us-by-the-green-lobby.

Shawn Lawrence Otto, "Waste-to-Energy Technology Is Cleaner and Safer than Generally Believed," MinnPost, June 6, 2013. http://www.minnpost.com/community-voices/2013/06/waste -energy-technology-cleaner-and-safer-generally-believed.

Brenda Platt, "Trash Incineration Isn't Renewable Energy," *Baltimore Sun*, May 10, 2011.

Neil Seldman, "Wasted Energy—Debunking the Waste-to-Energy Scheme," Institute for Local Self-Reliance, July 1, 2008. www .ilsr.org/commentary-wasted-energy-debunking-the-waste-to -energy-scheme.

Norman Steisel and Benjamin Miller, "Power from Trash," *New York Times*, April 28, 2010.

Alina Tugend, "Recycling Helps, but It's Not All You Can Do for the Environment," *New York Times*, October 19, 2012.

Gernot Wagner, "Going Green but Getting Nowhere," *New York Times*, September 8, 2011.

World Wildlife Fund, *The Energy Report: 100% Renewable Energy by 2015*, 2011. www.wwf.ca/conservation/global_warming/ener gy_report.cfm.

Websites

Earth911 (http://earth.911.com). Provides an array of simple yet effective tips for reducing waste via articles such as "41 Ways to Waste Less Today"; also offers ideas for reusing old products, information about what items are recyclable, and maps to iden-tify nearby recycling centers.

Greener Gadgets (www.greenergadgets.org). Teaches people how to choose the most environmentally friendly electronics and has a searchable database of electronics recycling centers by zip code; features energy tips, charts, videos, information on emerging green technologies, and an interactive calculator to see how much energy a household burns on the basis of its electronics usage.

GreenWaste (www.greenwaste.com). A private California company that collects, sorts, and recycles materials; has information about carpet recycling and composting, recycling statistics, puzzles, a glossary for students, and the downloadable *2012 Sustainability Report*.

Recycling Makes a Difference (www.recyclingmakesadifference .org). Offers a way for people to recycle their used cell phones, which recovers precious metals from them and keeps toxins out of the environment, and informs them about how they can donate the proceeds to a cause of their choice, such as planting trees, fighting hunger, conserving rain forests, and saving whales.

Use Less Stuff (www.use-less-stuff.com/). Offers research studies, archives of the monthly ULS Report, and the CalcuLess calculator to compare the environmental impact of various products— for example, the waste produced by a twelve-ounce drink bottle versus that of a six-ounce drink pouch.

INDEX

A

Aluminum recycling, 20, 27–28
  energy saved by, 27
  energy savings from, 32
American Economic Review (journal), 59
Annual Energy Outlook 2010 (US Energy Information Administration), 61

B

Baker, Rick, 25
Basel Action Network, 65
Benjamin, Daniel K., 17
Bloomberg, Michael, 7
Bornstein, David, 10

C

Climate change
  burning waste contributes to, 59–61
  recycling helps prevent, 32–34
Composting, 5–8
  amount of waste disposed by, by country, 54
  increases cost of waste disposal, 38
  waste-to-energy systems *vs.*, 58, 61
Curbside recycling
  costs of, 37, *37*

D

Danner, Jeff, 25
David, Joe, 51
Department of Energy, US, 49–50
Dual-stream recycling, 15

E

E-Stewards (recycling certification), 68
Eberlein, Sven, 6–7
Electronic waste (e-waste)
  amount exported to developing world, 65
  annual amount produced in US, 64
  percentage staying in US *vs.* exported, 69
  recycling of, 66
Electronics recycling, 66
  does not pollute third world countries, 64–69
  US jobs created by, 69
Energy Information Administration, US, 61
Energy subsidies, 18, 21

F

Fitch, George, 55, 56
Foster, Bill, 23, 25
France
  nuclear-fuel reprocessing plant in, 50

nuclear waste recycling in,
44–45

G
Glass recycling, 38
   environmental benefits of, *14*
Global Alliance for
   Incinerator Alternatives
   (GAIA), 57
Greenhouse gas emissions
   recycling reduces, 32–34
   from waste-to-energy plants
   vs. landfills, 60

H
Haber Stuart, 53–54
Hedlund, Mitch, 12, 15
Hickey, Laura, 15
Hiscott, Rebecca, 7

I
Independent Institute, 26
Institute of Scrap Recycling
   Industries, 40
International Trade
   Commission, US, 65

K
Kornell, Steve, 25

L
Landfill(s), 39
   amount of US waste disposed
   in, 11
   amount of waste disposed in,
   by country, *54*
   capacity is adequate, 36

Lilley, Floy, 35
Ludwig von Mises Institute,
   35

M
Metals recycling, 40
   energy savings from, 32
   environmental benefits of, *14*
Metcalf, Gordon, 21
Minter, Adam, 64
Mobro 4000 (garbage barge),
   17
Murphy, Laralyn, 26

N
Napolitano, Andrew, 8
National Recycling Coalition,
   31
National Wildlife Federation,
   15
New York Department of
   Conservation, 59
Newsom, Gavin, 6
Not-in-my-back-yard
   (NIMBY) syndrome, 36
Nuclear-fuel reprocessing
   plants(s), 50
Nuclear Non-Proliferation
   Treaty, 47–48
Nuclear waste
   container of, *44*
   countries recycling, *49*
   should be recycled, 41–45
   should not be recycled,
   47–50
Nuclear Waste Policy Act
   (1982), 42

O

Obama, Barack/Obama administration, 42, 52
Office of Technology Assessment, US, 39
Onondaga County Resource Recovery Agency, 55
Opinion polls. *See* Surveys

P

Paper recycling, 38
  does not save resources, 39
  energy savings from, 32
  environmental benefits of, *14*
PERC (Property and Environmental Research Center), 17
Plasco Energy Group, 55
Plastics recycling, 38
  does not save resources, 39
  energy savings from, 32
  environmental benefits of, *14*
Plutonium, 46–47
Polls. *See* Surveys
Pollution
  is minimal from new incinerator plants, 54–55
  recycling causes, 38–39
  recycling reduces, 32
  waste-to-energy plants create, 58–59, 63
  from waste-to-energy plants *vs.* landfills, *60*
Property and Environmental Research Center (PERC), 17

R

Recycle Across America (R.A.A.), 12
Recycling, *20*
  characteristics of people engaged in, *19*
  cost of, 20, *37*
  energy saved/greenhouse emissions reduced by, *33*
  environmental benefits of, *14*
  is necessary/effective, 10–16
  is unnecessary/ineffective, 17–21
  saves resources, 30–34
  should be mandatory, 22–25
  should not be mandatory, 26–29
  states with laws mandating, *24*
  waste-to-energy systems decrease rates of, 62
  wastes resources, 35–40
Reid, Harry, 42
Rodriguez, Guillermo, 5–6

S

San Francisco Mandatory Recycling and Composting Ordinance (2009), 5
Single-stream recycling, 13, 15
Solid Waste Association of North America, 38
South Carolina Department of Health and Environmental Control, 31

Stier, Jeff, 7
Surveys
  on disposal of e-waste, 65
  on support for nuclear waste
    recycling, *43*

T
Tampa Bay Times (newspaper), 22
Tax Policy and the Economy (journal), 21
Trash
  should be recycled into energy, 51–56
  should not be recycled into energy, 57–63

U
Union of Concerned Scientists (UCS), 46
United Nations Environment Program, 67
United States
  amount of energy wasted by not recycling waste in, 61
  annual amount of e-waste produced in, 64
  electronics recycling jobs created in, 69
  percentage of e-waste staying in, *vs.* exported, 69
  waste-to-energy/recycling/ landfilling rates in, *vs.* other countries, 54
Uranium, 48

V
Van Sickler, Michael, 23

W
Waste-to-energy plant(s), 53, 63
  emissions from, *vs.* landfills, 60
  percentage of waste disposed through, *vs.* recycling/landfilling, 54
Wolfram, Gary, 41

Y
Yucca Mountain (NV), 42, 44

PICTURE CREDITS